BRIDES FOR SALE?

BRIDES FOR SALE?

HUMAN TRADE IN NORTH YEMEN

EILEEN MACDONALD

MAINSTREAM
PUBLISHING

First published in Great Britain in 1988 by
MAINSTREAM   PUBLISHING   COMPANY
(EDINBURGH) LTD.
7 Albany Street
Edinburgh EH1 3UG

ISBN 1 85158 162 6 (cloth)
ISBN 1 85158 163 4 (paper)

British Library Cataloguing in Publication Data
MacDonald, Eileen
    Brides for sale?: human trade in north Yemen.
    1. (Arab Republic) Yemen. Brides. Sale.
    I. Title
    306.8'2

    ISBN 1-85158-162-6
    ISBN 1-85158-163-4 (paperback)

Typeset in Ehrhardt by EUSPB,
48 Pleasance, Edinburgh, EH8 9TJ.

Printed in Great Britain by Billings and Sons, Worcester

Contents

To Paul — never again.

ACKNOWLEDGEMENT

In the first place I am indebted to *The Observer* photographer Ben Gibson, who accompanied me in North Yemen. His photographs appear throughout this book, courtesy of *The Observer* newspaper. Angela Gordon, Robin Lustig, Donald Trelford and Tony McGrath are also due my gratitude. Jim Halley and his long-suffering wife Patricia have been invaluable in their help and inexhaustible patience. Finally, my sincere thanks go to Neila and her family for their courage.

Prologue

The girls stood framed in the doorway, holding the smaller children in their arms, while the boy clung to his mother's legs. The group seemed to sway, the girls covered from top to toe in Arab dress, their faces hidden by veils.

Zana, the elder, spoke, her strong Birmingham accent cutting through the shouting of the men in the room, silencing our interpreter. "We're ready. We are going to come with you. Will you take us home?"

I glanced at Ben Gibson, *The Observer* photographer who had flown with me from London to find these girls living in bleak and remote mountain villages in North Yemen. We had been told, only that morning, and in no uncertain terms, during a telephone call from the British Embassy, that if the villagers thought we were going to kidnap the girls, we would be shot. "Don't worry, we are not heroes," we had said then. But now we had just spent two hours with Zana and Nadia Muhsen, listening to their story.

At the ages of 15 and 14 years old respectively, the sisters from Sparkbrook in Birmingham had been married by their father to boys they had never seen who lived in backward, isolated mountain villages in the bandit area of North Yemen. In June 1980, Nadia was in her third year of secondary school, and Zana was filling in forms to be a nursery nurse. They were unaware, as were their mother, two younger sisters and brother, that they had just become brides.

Their father, who came from South Yemen, signed the marriage documents with the fathers of the boys, who were also living in Birmingham at the time. Then he told his daughters that he was going to give them a special treat — a six-week holiday to visit relatives in Yemen. He drew pictures of his homeland —

castles at the top of sand-dunes, people riding camels. Everyone was rich in Yemen, he told them. They would be staying on a farm and would be taught how to ride the camels. He did such a good job that his two younger daughters, then aged ten and 12, begged to be allowed to go too. "Later, when you are a little older," he told them.

He introduced his family to two male friends, who, he told them, had very kindly agreed to take the girls with them when they travelled to Yemen. Zana went first. The man she travelled with took her into the mountains to his village and introduced her to his son, aged 13. He told Zana she was married and she and his son would be sleeping together that night. "I screamed I couldn't be married. Daddy had only sent us on a holiday. Then the man told us he had paid £1,300 for me, and there was nothing I could do about it," Zana said.

She tried to warn her younger sister, who was due to arrive in two weeks, of what awaited her. But the letter she wrote home was taken from her by the man she had now to call her father-in-law. Nadia arrived with her father's friend, and was married to his son, then aged 12.

I had been aware of the facts of the story before meeting the sisters. In Birmingham I had met their mother, Miriam, who has battled for seven years to get her daughters home, and heard a tape-recording made by Zana and smuggled out of the village recounting what had happened to them.

I had thought that perhaps after seven years in the villages the girls would have adjusted to the way of life that had been thrust upon them. But nothing could be further from the truth. The first words Zana uttered when we arrived were: "We have been waiting for you. You have come to take us away, haven't you, please?"

And now, having talked to us about their life as well as they could, for they both seemed dazed, almost trance-like, the same plea again.

Ben and I asked our driver, a man I shall call Mohammed, if there was any way in which we could take the girls and their children in the jeep in which we had travelled. Mohammed, who had been unaware that we were journalists, and believed our story that we were doctors wishing to visit the girls while on holiday as we had presents from their relatives, shook his head and spoke rapidly to our interpreter, Neila, a half-British, half-Yemeni girl from London, who had been visiting relatives in Yemen when we met her by chance. Neila translated: "He says if only we had not travelled in the UNICEF jeep. He is known in these parts and if we took the girls away, he would be hunted down by the men of the mountains. They all know he works at the hospital and they could find him easily. He says he wants to do it, having heard their story, but there is no way — it would be suicide — not just for him but for all of us. They would never let us out of the mountains."

Just then one of the four men in the room with us, who understood English partially, began shouting. "You will not take our children. Take the girls, but leave the children."

The girls, who had seemed to turn to stone while we were discussing their future, suddenly went into action. Zana, shouting first in Arabic and then in English, said: "All right then, I will leave mine. I was raped anyway to get him. I will leave him."

But Nadia, her face twisted in pain, put a hand on her arm. "No," she said quietly. "We cannot leave our babies in this hell, not to this life of nothing." She held her daughter, Tina, 22 months, tightly in her arms. Her four-year-old son, Haney, stared from face to face.

The shouting of the men in the room — there were six of them — seemed to intensify and several got to their feet. Our driver, Mohammed, stood too, his hand on the Luger pistol tucked into his belt. Neila warned us that things could very quickly get out of control and suggested that someone fetch our supply of qat, the mild narcotic which everyone from government minister to peasant chews in Yemen, and which we had brought with us. When it was handed round, the steady chewing began, making the men look like so many Popeyes, with their bulging cheeks. Tempers cooled slightly and I was able to slip out of the room when Nadia beckoned me. She led me across the dark hall of the stone house, into a small bedroom. Inside was Zana, with a tear-streaked face. "We thought everyone had forgotten us," she said. "We have been waiting here for seven years for someone to come and take us home and we thought you were the ones."

I explained the difficulties we faced if we tried to smuggle the

Nadia and her daugher Tina, December 1987.

girls out of the mountain area, known as Mokbana, without the villagers' consent. The grapevine in the mountains which are dotted with tiny settlements would be alerted and we would be stopped on our way by road-blocks. The girls knew as well as I that the men of the mountains all carry guns, and do not hesitate to use them. On our way in, Ben and I had seen many village men, casually walking through the settlements with their Kalashnikovs slung over their shoulders. We had also been told that Mokbana was known as the area where the unwary and unwelcome simply disappear. A British expatriate, who said we must be mad to even consider entering the area, told us that there had been a census carried out recently in the whole of Yemen. Several information gatherers had gone into Mokbana, but none had returned. "The people in that area don't like strangers coming in and asking them about how many people live in a house or who is a relative of whom. Men are killed outright; women are killed in such a way that it looks like an accident."

Even if we had been able somehow to get the girls out of their village and past the immediately surrounding ones, we would face a 12-mile journey in the Land Rover which, because of the rough terrain and unmade road through Mokbana would take three hours before we reached the German-built tarmac road that would lead to Taiz, North Yemen's second city. Both our driver and Neila had warned us that in Mokbana it was essential to carry a gun — hence Mohammed's pistol. Neila, whose family have lived in Taiz for over 20 years, said no one enters Mokbana, known as the most dangerous region in Yemen, without at least one gun — even if the only purpose was for a picnic. She said: "Mokbana people are known for their violence. They are a complete law unto themselves. You carry a gun, and show you have it, just in case someone decides they should have your picnic basket and it would be safer if you were not around as a witness."

There was also the matter of "The Men of the Mountains", or to give them the name they are most widely known by in Yemen, "The Muslim Brothers", a fundamentalist group of Muslims who are feared by more moderate Yemenis. Neila told us, and it was confirmed in our conversation with both other expatriates and the sisters, that just behind Nadia's village was an army camp, filled by many Muslim Brothers. Neila also told us that the commander of the area was a Brother, known to have a fiery temper.

Even had we been able to negotiate the dirt track that served as a road through the high Mokbana mountains without bloodshed, and reached the tarmac road, we would have faced the road-blocks which are customary every 20 miles or less throughout North Yemen. These blocks are manned by soldiers bearing Kalashnikov rifles and, after ten in the morning, chewing qat and looking trigger-happy. Ben and I had passed through many in our four days in Yemen as tourists. But even tourists had to carry identification papers, special itinerary routes specifying who we were, where we had been and intended to go, and the length of stay in Yemen. Yemenis too had to present their identification papers at the road-blocks; Zana and Nadia had none, not even their passports, for these had been taken from them.

In the seven years they had been in Mokbana, they had only been outside the area a handful of times, and then only in an emergency — for example, the week before our visit, Nadia had been taken to Taiz to have her tonsils out. On every occasion, men from the village accompanied them. Zana told us: "They say we cannot travel outside because they are guilty and know we would try to run away if we were on our own. They have told us we can only travel if our husbands give us their permission — and they never do."

The lack of their spouses' permission was not entirely surprising. In common with many Yemenis, the girls' husbands did not live with their wives for the majority of the time. Both husbands had been working in Saudi Arabia for most of the seven years they had been married to Zana and Nadia. They had been home only twice — resulting in pregnancies both times — for a short stay of a month or so.

The girls had a plan which they thought might work. They would tell the village men that we were indeed friends of their mother who had come to visit. But their mother was very ill, and although she had managed to travel as far as Taiz, was too unwell to cross the mountains. She was begging to see her daughters and grandchildren before she died. The girls did try this story, but it was met with stony faces. The elder of the village, who under-stood a little English, said: "First we send someone to Taiz, to see how sick your mother is. Then if it is true, he comes back and takes you for a visit."

This gave birth to all sorts of crazy plans. Zana asked me if it would not be possible to fly their mother out and put her in a hospital in the town. But their mother had no visa for the country, and the risk to everyone was too great. The plan was finally discarded.

There seemed little else to do but leave, with the assurance that Ben and I would go straight to the British Embassy in the capital, Sana'a, to tell their story. We promised the sisters that help was going to come, and fast. They must hold on and be patient. "What do you think we have been doing for seven years?" asked Zana. "Patience is one thing we are perfect at."

Neila told them it was essential that they did not antagonise the villagers by saying they were going to leave. "If you keep saying that, they may move you to another village, somewhere so remote that there is not even a dirt track like the one here to reach you."

This was too much for Zana. "We can't keep quiet about leaving here. It is the only thing we ever talk about and we dream about it too. My mother-in-law likes to tease me. She says: 'You think you are going to heaven, to England. But you are not. You never will see it again. You are going to stay here forever with us in hell.' When she says that to me, and particularly after you have been today, I say to her: 'I am going home to my mummy and my friends.' It is the only thing that keeps us sane, saying it over and over to them."

For such talk, and any behaviour considered rebellious, the sisters had often been beaten. They were beaten when they arrived and cried for home, when they refused to sleep with their boy-husbands, when they refused to write "happy letters" home and make a tape-recording saying they were enjoying Yemen. Zana was repeatedly punished because she would stay for a few minutes extra at her sister's house in the evening. They were also beaten when they found it impossible at first to get used to the heavy workload of Yemeni wives — rising at four in the morning, working in the fields, fetching water from the well, sometimes miles away, and carrying it home on their heads without spilling a drop. Even when pregnant they had to work in the fields until labour pains began, then they would crawl into a hut to give birth, aided by old women. And the next morning, with the baby at the breast, they would be back in the fields again.

They had got used to all this, spoke and wrote fluent Arabic, even appeared as Yemeni women, yet clung fiercely to the hope they would be rescued. "When my son was born, they called him Mohammed. I call him Marcus, just to spite them. They don't like it, they hit me sometimes, but I don't care. When you've gone I am going to tell them they haven't got long. That help is on its way for us, and they are going to pay for what they've done to us."

Nothing we could say would convince Zana to do otherwise, so we prepared to leave. Neither she nor Nadia, much the quieter of the two girls, could bear to climb down the mountain to where our UNICEF jeep had been left because the dirt track had finally ended its struggle up the almost vertical rock-face.

We said goodbye to the sisters and their children inside the little stone house that clung to the mountain in the village of Ashube. Most of the village had come to see us off, and the children, sure-footed as goats, ran ahead, down the pathway. When we reached the jeep, Ben thought it would be a good idea to take photographs of everyone around it, fitting in with our cover-story of being tourists visiting relatives of friends. Everyone wanted to take the picture and be in it at the same time.

Eventually we climbed in and started back towards civilisation. The meeting of the afternoon had been exhausting, the tension at times unbearable. We were all talking, thinking of how we could get the girls home, when suddenly, in front of us, a jeep appeared coming hell for leather towards ours. The track would not allow two jeeps to pass. We saw the other stop, effectively blocking our way.

Armed men got out and came towards us, their hands fingering their rifles. There was a lot of shouting in Arabic, to which both Neila and Mohammed answered in kind. Neila, who was sitting next to me in the front of the jeep said: "They want to know why we have visited the girls. I have told them you are just friends, and asked why the guns if they have nothing to hide. One of them says he is an uncle of the girls, and that he will not allow them to leave. I told him if he feels so guilty about the girls why he is behaving like this, why doesn't he lock them up and put chains on their legs? He didn't like that. He said that Yemen is a free country and no one imprisons the women."

It was a nail-biting ten minutes for Ben and me, understanding nothing of the shouting and gestures, except those words which Neila was interpreting. At one point two men started circling the jeep, peering in at the back to where Ben sat on the ice-box. Finally, and reluctantly, they waved us on; Ben, with more nerve than I, waving back to them and offering to take their photographs in true tourist style.

As Mohammed started the jeep and we drove on, Neila laughed. "They were sure we had the girls somewhere, but even they could see they weren't in the ice-box. They know they have done wrong and that people are interested in the girls or they would not be so aggressive."

Another mile or so further on, and the same thing happened, only this time it was in a village, and not just a jeep blocked our way, but several dozen people, some of whom seemed intent on getting inside our jeep, just to check it out. Again, Neila and Mohammed shouted back, telling the villagers they were giving tourists a bad impression by making such a fuss. We were told we could continue on our way.

The rest of the journey passed uneventfully, and we could hardly believe our luck when we saw the tarmac road after three gruelling hours. For Ben and I the priority was to get to the Embassy in the capital, but after such a day we both felt it could wait until morning. If we had only known, as we celebrated the comparative ease with which we had got in and out of Mokbana, and the tremendous story we had for the newspaper that Sunday, that the commander of the villages in Taiz had that afternoon been alerted that two journalists were in his area, looking for the girls, and had issued orders that we should be picked up immediately.

Chapter One

Zana Muhsen was born on 7 July 1964, her sister, Nadia, on 13 October the following year. They had few advantages in life, apart from the fierce love of their mother. The first few years of their lives were spent in a rundown suburb of Birmingham in a series of one-room homes with their mother, Miriam Ali, and father, Muthana Muhsen.

When Zana was two years old and Nadia just one, their father, originally from Yemen, announced he was going to take their elder brother and sister home to his family for a holiday. Miriam knew better than to argue, although she protested that Leila, only five, and Ahmed, four, were too young to travel so far. Muthana regularly hit her, although her own upbringing had prepared her for that.

Born of an English mother and Pakistani father, she had been persistently battered and abused as a child when her own father died and her mother moved in with a white Englishman. Nine children had followed, and from the age of four, Miriam had looked after her younger half brothers and sisters, enduring the beatings from her stepfather and his favourite name for her, "Paki bastard". At the age of 17, Miriam met Muthana, who was living in the same lodging house in King's Heath, Birmingham. He told her he was from Aden in South Yemen and that, as a 15-year-old, he had run away from home and fled to England because he had been forced into an arranged marriage by his family in the village of Marais.

The couple moved in together, and Muthana, who had virtually no money started, according to Miriam, to claim for fictitious children and do "a bit of wheeling and dealing", to supplement his dole money. They were living in rented accommodation, and sleeping on floorboards. When Miriam timidly suggested they could get married, he hit her and said he was claiming on his income tax forms that she was his housekeeper.

Leila was born in 1961, and from that time on Muthana kept Miriam at home, accusing her of being a prostitute if she said she wanted to go out to visit friends. "At first, I thought I loved him. He could be very charming, but he used to hit me too," said Miriam, who is now 44. "One day I hit him back, and he stopped, he was so surprised. I stuck with him hoping he would change, and to give my babies a father. He would not let me out of the house. He said it was the woman's place to stay in the home. I only had one friend, a nurse who lived round the corner. Muthana only let me see her because I lied to him and said she was a cousin."

Muthana took his two older children to Marais, in Aden, and stayed nine months, never sending word back to Miriam. She was living in one room of a three-storey Victorian house which was full of bedsits, mainly occupied by Arab lodgers. "They seemed to think that because I was on my own with the two children, I was fair game. At night I had to barricade the door because they would try to get in."

When Muthana finally did come home, it was without the children. Miriam was hysterical, then dumbfounded at what he had done. "He said he had left them with his father. He said his father had a big, beautiful house in Marais and the children had wanted to stay with their grandad. I said how could they know, they were only babies, and I tried everything I knew to get them back. I wrote to the Foreign Office, and to the Home Office, saying they had to get my babies home. But all I got was cold letters back, saying the children, because of their father, were of dual nationality — both British and Yemeni — and that in Yemen, where they were now, they would be considered Yemeni citizens. I tried for two years to get them home, then I was pregnant again, and made myself believe the children would be all right."

Miriam had three more children after Zana and Nadia: Aisha, Tina and Mohammed. She brought them all up as Christians, as she herself had been reared. Muthana, she says, although a

Muslim, was entirely irreligious and displayed no concern over either his or his children's religion. She devoted herself to them, and admits she spoiled them, because their father at his best ignored them, at his worst would try to beat them.

"He used to try hitting them, but never when I was there because he knew I would flatten him," said Miriam, who is five feet, one inch tall. "For some reason he particularly had it in for Aisha. I attacked him once because she had brushed against his legs in the hallway — she was only about three and he hit her. Most of the time, though, he just pushed them out of his way, he was not interested in them; I used to have to nag him for days for money to buy the children's birthday presents. I used to envy my nurse friend because her husband was a good man and loved his children. He would spend time with them, talking and playing with them.

"One of the few things Muthana would let me do was take the children out occasionally to the park. Then I would just stand and stare at the dads playing with their children on the swings, and think: 'If only I had a man like that.'

"My friend was able to go out any time she liked — to the shops, or to Bingo. She was married to a Muslim, but a good man. Muthana used to accuse me of trying to go with other men if I asked to go out. He never did any work himself — just would go out drinking then come home and shout at me. I was like a prisoner, looking after the kids, trying to keep whichever room we were living in tidy, and cooking his meals."

The family moved into a house that Muthana bought in Goldenhillock Road, Small Heath, Birmingham. He could not afford the mortgage, so let out all of the rooms to lodgers. Miriam complained about trying to live with four young children in what was virtually a hallway, sharing the kitchen and bathroom with strangers, so Muthana built an "extension" off the kitchen to house his family.

Miriam's friend, nurse Anne Sufi, remembers it well. "We used to call it 'the shed'. Muthana built it out of old bits of wood he found lying around. It was literally just tacked together. The whole family slept, ate and lived in that room. He wouldn't give Miriam any rooms in the house for the family because he could not afford the mortgage. He said the rooms were for lodgers only.

The shed was under six feet high. There was no damp course, nothing. Miriam slept on a bed-settee with the four kids and it was heated with a calor gas stove. It was beyond belief really."

Anne remembers that Muthana was seldom at home when she called on the family. "For some time he worked at a couple of factories, or else he would be out with his Yemeni friends in Birmingham. He had a couple of accidents and got around £16,000 but his family never saw any of it. He would leave Miriam five shillings on the mantelpiece in the kitchen. This would be the late sixties, and that amount of money to feed, clothe and buy things for four children did not go very far at all. Miriam took it all at that stage. She kept saying: 'Maybe he'll change.'

"When Muthana did come into the shed and found me there he was not happy at all. But because he believed I was Miriam's cousin and knew I was married to a Muslim, he would just scowl and leave me and Miriam talking."

Anne, like Miriam, admitted that Muthana Muhsen could be "very charming" at times. "Occasionally, one of the children would come into my house, showing off a new coat that their dad had bought. But he really was not interested in them."

Miriam recalled that Muthana's chief interest in life at the time seemed to be attending meetings of the Palestine Liberation Organisation, and talking politics with other Arabs. She vividly remembers a cold day in London when Muthana took his family to their first political rally in Trafalgar Square. "He just dumped us in a café, and off he went with his friends," she said. "We sat there all day. I did not know London then, or I would have tried to get home on the train."

She thinks that because of his outspokenness, Muthana is on a "death list" in communist South Yemen. "I remember several Yemenis in Birmingham telling me his name had been put on a list because of his views, and that if he ever went back to South Yemen he would be dead."

The end of life in the shed came when a neighbour reported Muthana to the planning department and rates office in Birmingham. No planning permission had ever been sought and a public health inspector called and condemned the structure as unsafe. Muthana was given seven days to pull it down.

He bought a fish and chip shop at 166 Stratford Road in the rundown Birmingham suburb of Sparkbrook and moved Miriam and the children into the upstairs accommodation. Miriam was expected to run the shop, while Muthana went to talk politics to his friends. She remembers it as one of the worst periods of her life. "I was trying to bring up the four kids, keep them clean and run the shop, which became a sort of café for the kids in the district. Muthana hated the black people in the area. He used to say that in Yemen they were kept as slaves, but he didn't mind them filling the shop all day when they should have been at school. The public health inspectors used to visit it regularly and complain about the conditions in the kitchen. Muthana would get into trouble, and then blame it on me."

By now Zana and Nadia had started to attend St Albans Church of England School in Highgate. Nadia, a withdrawn child at home, quickly became known as the terror of the school. Headmistress, Miss Sheila Lyman, remembers her as the worst pupil the school ever had, before or since. "I was deputy head when Nadia was here, and it was part of my job to talk to disruptive pupils. I spent an awful lot of time with Nadia.

"We were at our wits' end with her. In desperation we put her in with a first year class to try and shame her into behaving. It worked, but only for a week. If she had stayed here she would have been a prime candidate for a Pre-Suspension Unit, or suspension.

"Zana and the younger sisters could be naughty too. But they all had pleasant personalities. They were a very close family, very close in particular to their mother and, when the girls went, Aisha and Tina were extremely upset. I think they were frightened too, that their father might do the same thing to them. They became even closer to their mother. Just from the way they behaved towards their mother, I knew that neither Zana nor Nadia would have willingly left her to go to live in Yemen.

"I remember seeing their mother some time after the girls had gone. I couldn't believe it was the same woman. She used to be very big — she looked half her size."

Miss Lyman has never met Muthana. "It was always the mother, whom we knew as Mrs Muhsen, who came to the school if there was a problem or a parents' night or to attend the school play. Sometimes she said she would tell their father about bad behaviour, but I never knew if the message got through."

The school suggested Nadia be moved to another nearer her home. Miriam demurred. She said: "Nadia was not really as bad as they made out. She was bullied a lot at school and was very unhappy. It was so bad for her that she asked if she could be put in a classroom on her own, but they refused. She was always very quiet, and I think she was picked on."

Whichever version is nearer the truth, Nadia was soon in trouble outside school. At the age of 13, she was arrested for theft and fined £90. A social worker was assigned to the family. Miriam who, according to her friends, can see no wrong in any of her children, claims her arrest was unjustified.

"We were in the market, and I was at one stall while Nadia was looking at some jewellery on another. She picked up a ring, and was walking over to me, holding it up and saying, 'Mum, can I have this?' when the stallholder grabbed her and called the police. I told him it was a mistake, but the police came and took her away. They locked her up. I was with her in court and afterwards I went over to the man and tried to hit him, but was dragged off. I was there on my own, Muthana didn't want to know."

The court case was to become the crunch factor for Muthana in deciding to marry off Nadia. In November 1987, after weeks of denying that he had arranged their marriages, he admitted to it, saying he was dissatisfied with their behaviour. Recently he added: "They were wrecking my family name. She (Nadia) was in court as a thief and she had my name." He gave further reasons: "Everyone was saying to me that my daughters were going out with blacks. I was very ashamed. If they had stayed here in Birmingham, they would have married a black or become prostitutes. I had to save my name."

Muthana's racism is well known among friends of the family. Mrs Anne Sufi said: "He really hated black people. He was terrified that his daughters were going to go out with a black boy. I don't know what colour he thought he was. And if Nadia or any of the others were naughty, it was because of their home life, cooped up with their mother in bad accommodation, with a father coming in drunk and shouting. He seems to have taken no responsibility at all for his children. I remember him saying to me and my husband once, when we said he should treat Miriam better, that it was her job as a woman to stay in the home and look after the children. He was a man and had more important things to do."

Muthana has also alleged that neither of his daughters were virgins when he sent them to Yemen. Mrs Muriel Wellington, whose daughter, Lynette, was Zana's best friend, said: "None of his kids had a chance to sleep with anyone, he never let them out of the house. When Lynette and the other girls were going to discos, Zana was never allowed, even though Miriam thought it would do them good, and was a perfectly natural thing for youngsters to do. Muthana thought she would dance with a black boy and then go to bed with him.

"Sometimes Zana would come here with Lynette and listen to records. But even then Miriam would be terrified in case Muthana found out she wasn't at home and would turn nasty. I was always bumping into Miriam in Sparkbrook looking for one of the kids because Muthana might come home and create if they were not all there. They were all like prisoners, really."

Aisha, Miriam's fourth daughter, now aged 21, and the mother of a three-year-old girl by her black boyfriend told how her father's black paranoia extended to the ice-rink. "Even when we were little kids, he would not let us have black friends. He used to say that we couldn't go ice- skating because black boys may be there. The only thing he let us do was go to the Youth Club. He liked to know just where we were all the time.

"We used to try to love him, because he was our dad, even though he didn't act like our friends' fathers. When we played with our friends and they told us about their dads, and how they went out together, we would get upset and ask mum why our dad didn't like us. We felt we ought to like him, but after what he has done to Zana and Nadia we all hate him.

"I used to go round with Zana and Nadia, we were together always. They were just normal girls, we weren't bad, or prostitutes or anything. If you knew the sort of life we had you would know it was impossible for us to have behaved like that, even if we wanted to which we certainly didn't. I really miss them and get very upset sometimes.

"When our mum found out what he had done to them, she left him and took us. We were all scared he might do the same to us.

After we left him, Tina and me used to go to discos and we would see our father there with his girlfriends. It would make us sick. He had been so strict with us, but there he was, our dad, with these young girls. He got girls for his men-friends too. Sometimes we would see him drive past in a hired car with girls and men in the back. He had loads of them, but whenever we happened to be at the same disco, he would turn his back on us."

Her younger brother, Mohammed, 15, added: "I want to kill him and if my sisters don't come home, I will."

Mrs Wellington, a widow, said: "If only Muthana had realised it, he had lovely children. They have a special closeness, maybe because they feel it is them against the world. I don't know how any father could accuse his own daughters of being prostitutes, particularly Zana and Nadia. Zana, for example, told me she wanted to be a nun. She was always covered up, from head to toe. I don't think I ever saw her legs. They wanted to love their father, but he was not interested in them."

Chapter Two

Suddenly Muthana began to take an interest in his children — at least in Nadia.

He began talking of his homeland, the village where he had been born, Marais, and the mountain area of Mokbana, in North Yemen. Aisha, then 12 years old, remembers him speaking of castles in the sand, barebacked horse-riding and camels. "He even sat down at the table one day and started drawing pictures of these wonderful castles built on sand-dunes," she said. "We thought it sounded great. He said that everyone was rich in Yemen and his parents had a big farm which was green and lush. Then he asked Nadia if she wanted to go on holiday there, for six whole weeks. She was over the moon, and the rest of us were very jealous of her."

Shortly before this, one of Muthana's friends, Gohad Abdul Majid, also originally from Yemen, began to regularly visit the family, also telling stories of the beauty of his home country. He took a special interest in Nadia. He showed her photographs of his family who lived in a village in Mokbana. One was a photograph of his son, Mohammed, then aged about 14. Miriam said: "We had known Gohad for years, as one of Muthana's friends. We respected him because he was an old friend of his. When he showed the photographs we all just took a polite interest, as they were his relations. He said that he would be going home in June, and that if Nadia wanted to go on holiday, he would accompany her on the flight, and take her to visit his family in the village. He seemed to be genuinely putting himself out to help her have a nice holiday, and as I say, I trusted him, because I had known him for years."

Miriam was very keen for her daughter to have the holiday for several reasons. "She had been having a very bad time, what with the court business and school. I thought a good holiday would cheer her up and give her a new outlook on things. I was amazed at Muthana suddenly becoming generous and suggesting the holiday. Now I know he didn't pay for it — Gohad did, and that wasn't out of kindness either. He was taking his daughter-in-law to his son."

Because of Nadia's conviction, Miriam had to get the written permission of her social worker, which was gladly given. The school, too, were delighted. Miriam had to ask the headmistress to sign Nadia's photographs for her passport. Miss Lyman commented: "We were very glad about this good long holiday for Nadia. We hoped it might do the trick and she would come back to school in the autumn term a different girl because, quite honestly, if she had gone on the way she was we would have had to suspend her. We thought that an exotic holiday could be the answer — give her something to enjoy, get her away from her old environment and help her mature. She was bound to learn something anyway, having travelled a bit and met people of a different culture and way of life."

Nadia herself was wildly excited. The family had never been on a holiday before, and she was delighted to have been chosen. All the children were jealous, Zana the most, and she began pleading to be able to go with her sister. She had just left school, and had decided to be a nursery nurse. A holiday, like the one her younger sister was going on, would be the adventure of a lifetime, and a wonderful break before she started on her career.

One night their father came home with even more good news. He had decided that Zana too should be allowed to go on the holiday. He had met another old Yemeni friend of his living in Birmingham, Mohammed Abdul Khada. He would be going home for a holiday in a few weeks, and had agreed to take Zana as a favour to his old friend, Muthana. Zana was now able to score over Nadia — she would be going first, also to Mokbana, but to a village about a mile from where Nadia would be staying, even higher in the mountains.

The plan was agreed. Zana would travel with Mr Khada in June, and spend her 16th birthday thousands of miles away in exotic, rich Yemen riding barebacked on horses and camels.

Nadia would follow two weeks later, and the sisters would stay together in one of the villages, then, with a relation of one of their father's kind friends, travel all over Yemen having the time of their lives for six whole weeks.

Their father arranged everything. Now the neglected family began to have a different view of him. Miriam thought the worm had changed. "I thought I had been right all along to stick with him. If he could send my girls on this wonderful holiday then he couldn't be all bad. I thought maybe everything would be different with him now he was interested in his children and prepared to do all this for them."

In a high state of excitement, Zana started packing. Her mother was worried about the sort of clothes she would have to take and what would be considered suitable for a Muslim country. Muthana told her: "Just the clothes she has. Yemen is open to Western ideas about dress."

Ashube, December 1987.

Zana left in June with Mr Khada, promising to send postcards home. They flew to the North Yemen capital, Sana'a, reputed to be the most ancient and beautiful city of the Arab world, teeming with mosques and markets. Zana wanted to go shopping, but Mr Khada insisted they travel straight to Taiz to stay with some of his relatives. They were anxious to meet her, he said.

It was a long but spectacular journey by bus, down through the centre of the country, through high mountain passes, along narrow, tortuous roads that offered precipice drops.

On their arrival in Taiz, North Yemen's second city, Mr Khada took Zana to stay with some relatives. They treated her courteously, but seemed reluctant to show her the sights, or even for her to go browsing in the markets. They also seemed to spend most of their time talking in corners, and Zana could see from the way they would nod towards her they were talking about her. She thought they were just curious to see a Western girl in her pencil-skirt and blouse. At that time, and even today, the tourist industry has still not really taken hold in the country. At Mr Khada's suggestion, she wrote a couple of postcards home, saying she was having a wonderful time.

After a few days, Zana began to get bored of this hanging around in the house. She had come for the adventure of her lifetime and was anxious to be able to show off to Nadia when she arrived about the things she had already done. Sitting in a stone room on a mattress was not going to impress anyone.

Finally, however, Mr Khada told her that in the morning they were going to visit his village in the mountains, about three hours or so drive away. They would have to hire a jeep because the mountain road was very rough. Sure enough, very early in the morning, Zana was shaken awake by one of the women in the house. She got dressed, picked up her small suitcase and jumped into the back of the jeep.

They drove out of Taiz for about an hour, then turned right on the road leading to the mountains. As they bumped along, Zana kept imagining the wonderful welcome the villagers were going to give her. She doubted they had ever seen a Western girl before and she was going to enjoy it all immensely. She might even teach them English, she thought, and perhaps she would learn to speak what appeared to her their incomprehensible language.

The jeep finally stopped after a couple of hours. It was ten o'clock in the morning and already stiflingly hot. Mr Khada told her that they were about halfway up Mount Ala Sharub. His village was right at the top, and they would have to walk. It was, Zana remembers, a very gruelling trek, which seemed to take forever in the heat.

The village, when they reached it, was a disappointment. Mr Khada told her it was called Hockail, and it was very near Ashube, where Nadia was going to visit. Nobody was really about to welcome her — she had expected to be mobbed by excited children. A few women, carrying water jugs on their heads, stopped to stare at her. Ragged, barefoot children stood with fingers in their mouths. Little girls, looking only about six years old, but carrying water or brushwood, like their mothers, averted their eyes. The men of the villages, squatting on their haunches and chewing qat, waved and shouted to Mr Khada, ignoring his companion.

Mr Khada led Zana into a stone house with cement floors. It was very dark and cold inside, with tiny windows, and no electricity. On the roof was a kitchen of sorts — a dark, cockroach-infested room with a stone fireplace on which meals were cooked. This was his father's house he told her and led her upstairs to a long, low room. Two elderly people got off the mattresses on the floor to greet him. The old woman stroked Zana's hair, and smiled at Mr Khada, chattering in Arabic. One of the children, a boy who looked about ten years old to Zana, ran into the house and Mr Khada bent to embrace him. Zana, feeling rather out of things and wishing she could at least understand the language, stood to one side until, after a few minutes, Mr Khada seemed to remember his guest's presence. He took her upstairs to a small, dark room in which were two mattresses. "This is your room," he told her. "When your sister comes, she will share it with you."

That night, Zana was left alone while downstairs the family talked and laughed together. Through her tiny window she could see the stars and hear cows and sheep, the occasional bleat of a goat. This, she thought, was the real start of her holiday.

In the morning, she got up and washed. That was one thing about this holiday she was not at all keen on — the sanitary conditions. A hole in the ground served as the toilet. One of Mr Khada's female relations had shown it to her — in the basement of the house. There was no running water, but a jug of water for the use of the whole family stood at the back of the house.

After she had made herself presentable, and wishing she had brought looser clothes because of the heat, Zana went in search of Mr Khada to find out what had been planned for her to do. She found him in the downstairs room, and he beckoned her over. He asked if she liked Yemen, and she said: "Very much, thank you." Then, as she sat beside him, he said bluntly: "You are going to stay here with us. You are married."

Zana laughed: "No, I am not. I am not married. You know that — and I am not staying here, it is only a holiday."

He said: "You are married. Your father has arranged it."

At this point in recounting her story, Zana remembers little, except that she had hysterics. "I screamed: 'I can't be married. I am on holiday.' He just stared at me. I screamed and screamed. I remember saying: 'Who am I married to?' and he pointed to his son, that little puny kid, and said: 'Mohammed. You are my son's wife.' I wanted to faint, and scream and wake up. I knew it must be a nightmare, and that I would wake up and find Mummy standing over me and I would be in my bed above the fish and chip shop. Abdul Khada shook me and said there was nothing I could do, it had all been fixed in Birmingham, and he had the marriage certificate, and my birth certificate. He said he had paid £1,300 to my father for me, and that Mr Majid had paid the same for Nadia.

"I couldn't believe it. I couldn't believe my father was that wicked. I couldn't believe any of it. Then he called his son over. You should have seen him. He was much smaller than me; he was only 14. Abdul Khada spoke to him and the boy kept nodding and not saying much. He was scared of me. Then Abdul Khada said to me that I would be sleeping with Mohammed that night. I was screaming and shaking and I said 'NO, never.' Then Abdul Khada said: 'You'd better, otherwise the village women will hold you down so he can get up and climb on you.' I really don't remember much more — except it was awful. I was in shock. I thought my mummy must have arranged it too. I felt I could never again trust anyone. I wanted to kill myself. I don't remember that night, except that it happened. That boy had sex with me. I was raped."

The next morning, Zana was shaken awake by a woman who she now realised was her mother-in-law — Mr Khada's wife. In accordance with the custom of many Yemeni men, Mr Khada had left her in the village while he went to work in England. He had last seen his son when he was about four years old. Now he had returned with his son's bride, who although she may be a bit troublesome at first would soon settle down, learn the language and the chores and lifestyle befitting a Yemeni wife.

First things first. Zana's own clothes were taken away, and her mother-in-law pointed to a pile of Arab clothes and a head-dress. Numbed, Zana· put them on. Her mother-in-law showed her what was expected of her — walking, climbing and falling down the mountain to reach the well for water; how to carry the jar on her head, to work in the fields, tend to the cows and goats; how to make bread by putting her hand in the fire to turn the chapatis in the flames. She had also to keep the whole house clean and learn how to cook Yemeni food. Zana began to understand that she was little more than a slave, and to avoid blows it was better to obey. Her husband, whom she despised, and whom she could not even communicate with, seems to have been equally subservient to the requests of his parents. "He didn't want me, but he was scared of his father. He slept with me at night, but kept away during the day. It all just happened. I did not seem to have any control any more. It was like living on another planet. Birmingham seemed miles away. I didn't think I was me any more — Zana Muhsen from Sparkbrook seemed somebody else."

Zana cannot remember how many days her trance lasted. But one morning she realised she would have to warn Nadia that the same fate awaited her. She had paper and a pen with her and wrote a letter home to Sparkbrook. "'Don't come, Nadia,' I wrote, 'they are going to marry you here in this hell. They have got me — that is enough.'" But Mr Khada discovered the letter and took it from her. He said he would post it, but it never got to England.

In late June, Nadia travelled from Birmingham with Mr Gohad Abdul Majid. With her she carried birthday presents and cards from the family and Zana's schoolfriends. She was taken by

Ahmed, December 1987.

Mr Khada to Taiz, to meet her sister, who was staying at another
house in the city . Neither girl can remember much of that
meeting — except tears and despair. Zana recalled catching hold
of her sister's hand and whispering, "Nadia, I've got to tell you
something, but you must promise not to cry. You're married."
When they were left alone, they tried to think of ways of escape,
but with no money and no passports — for the men had taken
them from both girls — they were trapped. "I told Nadia what
was going to happen, but she wouldn't believe me. She said it
must be a mistake, and we would write home, asking to go back
at once. But the men just laughed at us. When I screamed then,
Abdul Khada just hit me. He had started to hit me a lot, whenever
he felt like it.

"When we got back to my village, they took Nadia away. She
was crying. It was awful. She was only 14. They took her to
Ashube, and the same thing happened to her with Gohad's
family. The boy she was forced to sleep with was only 13. He
didn't want to and Gohad hit him to make him. They didn't like
us seeing too much of each other; they used to hit us and make
us work. We were like slaves.

"We kept asking to be allowed to write letters to Mummy, but
they said, 'Not yet.' They said they would let us write home, but
they would tell us what to put. They said they would hit us if we
did not do as we were told. I can't tell you how scared we were of
them. They said our father had sold us to them, and now they had
to do everything they told us. We just didn't know what they
might do next. We were petrified. They said we would have to
make a tape-recording saying that we were very happy. They
would send it home to Daddy, and if anyone asked him about us,
he could play it to prove he was a good father and that we liked
Yemen and loved our husbands and were good wives."

Meanwhile, in Sparkbrook, Miriam was wondering why she
had not received any more postcards from her daughters, beyond
those which Zana had sent at the beginning of her holiday. She
supposed they were either having such a wonderful time that they
had forgotten to send any, or that the postal service in North
Yemen was very slow.

Muthana, who had never before been a heavy drinker, now
seemed permanently drunk, even though as far as she knew he

was not working, and certainly the shop was doing no better than it had for years. She asked him where he got all the money from to drink so much, but got no answer. She continued to run the fish and chip shop, and to look after her younger children, all complaining that they had not had a holiday and wanted to go away. "Next year," Muthana told his younger daughters.

In spite of his surliness, Miriam felt grateful to Muthana. On Zana's 16th birthday in July, she imagined her daughters having a wonderful time, singing and dancing with their new Yemeni friends. When anyone came into the shop, she would recount what a fantastic time the girls must be having. After years of doing without, and being very much the poor woman who lived with Muthana Muhsen and slaved over her children, Miriam Ali felt she had something to boast about.

Nadia, Tina and Zana, December 1987.

Chapter Three

Miriam was serving in the shop one day in the middle of July when some schoolfriends of her daughters came in. "Hey, Miriam," one of them said. "Your Zana and Nadia have got married."

Miriam's first reaction was: "Don't be silly. They are on holiday. You know that." But the girls persisted — a British woman in Sparkbrook, married to a Yemeni from Mokbana, had just heard the news.

"I started shaking," said Miriam. "Then I asked them for the address of the woman and ran round there. The woman answered the door and I said who I was, and asked if it was true. 'Yes,' she said. 'My husband has just got back from there and he says they got married last month.' I ran back home, I was in such a state, I didn't know what had happened. I kept saying to myself: 'It can't be true. They are coming home soon. It's a mistake.'"

She found Muthana in the shop and, in tears, asked him if there was any truth in the news. "No," he said. "They are on holiday, that's all."

"I didn't believe him. I asked him what he had done. Those men were his friends, and if anything had happened to the girls, they must be behind it. He got angry and started shouting. 'I've done nothing,' he said. 'My friends are good men, nothing has happened to my daughters.'"

For three days Miriam hammered away at him, convinced he was lying. More people, mainly from the Yemeni community, told her the news was true. They also told her that Muthana had sold his daughters to his friends. "I felt in my bones he was lying to me, I knew he had married them off and, although I had no proof, and it wasn't until later I was definitely told he had sold them, I knew he had. Finally, one evening, Muthana, on the way out to the pub, told the truth. 'They went over there and they met nice boys. They are the sons of my two friends, and they got married. Now they are going to be respectable Yemeni women instead of going out with blacks and becoming prostitutes.'"

Miriam grabbed his arm as he was about to leave. "What have you done?" she screamed. "You knew all along. Those photographs of Gohad's son — you fixed it with them, didn't you?"

She recalled the scene. "I had grabbed him, and I wasn't going to let him go until he told me the truth. He was scared of me in that mood — I was a big woman then, very strong. He told me to shut up — that his friends were downstairs and might hear. Then he admitted what he had done — married them off behind my back. He said the arrangement had been made at a house in Birmingham earlier in the year.

"He said Gohad and Abdul Khada were present at the ceremony. He must have got the girls' birth certificates out of my drawer when I was downstairs in the shop. They had got the marriage documents from somewhere, he said. He wouldn't tell me where, but he said they were legal and stamped. There had been two witnesses, both Yemeni men living near us. He wouldn't tell me who they were.

"When he told me he had signed the certificates, I screamed: 'How could you, they are my babies! They are mine. They are your daughters, and you sold them.' He smiled at me and said: 'Prove it.' I said: 'I am going to get them back.' Then he laughed in my face, and said: 'You try it. There is nothing you can do. They are gone, like the other two.'

"I just went mad. I had been ironing, and I let go of him to pick up the ironing board. He was trying to get out of the door and I smashed it across his back. I said I was going to kill him, and I meant it. It broke and he ran out, shouting that he would pay me back. Then I sat down and went to pieces. I thought what my girls must be thinking, that I had let them go. I thought about my other two children out there, I cried for them too. I had no idea if they were alive or dead. I had tried to get them back and failed, but there was no way I was going to give up on Zana and Nadia. If it killed me I was going to get them home."

For the next few days, Miriam was too shell-shocked to do anything. Aisha remembers her mother being too dazed to talk, and herself scarcely believing that their father had married off her sisters. Then 12 years old, she remembers coming in from school one day to find her mother crying. "I started to cry too. I said: 'Never mind, Mum, I am going to write them a letter, telling them they have got to come home at once.' I sat down at the table and started to write, but Dad came in and asked me what I was doing. I said that my sisters weren't happy, and he shouted that they were. Then he grabbed my letter and tore it up."

Letters started to arrive from the girls saying they were happy and begging their mother not to worry. But Miriam noticed that Muthana only allowed her to read some of the mail from her daughters. Other letters from them he kept in his jacket pocket. Miriam suspected these told a different story, but was too frightened to look in case he caught her rummaging through his clothes and beat her up.

Muthana, arriving home drunk one night, raped Miriam. She suffered a nervous breakdown, from which she has never really recovered. She went to her doctor and was given tranquillizers. She told him she could no longer go on living with Muthana — that either she would kill herself, or him. The doctor, in conjunction with the social services, managed to find a new home for Miriam, Aisha, Tina and Mohammed. It was in Queen's Avenue, King's Heath, about a mile from the fish and chip shop. Although it was run down, Miriam moved in on the same day.

Muthana was left to run the fish and chip shop on his own. He assured anyone who would listen that the girls were happy, and that he would shortly be getting more letters to prove it. Miriam wouldn't see him. In fact she has only seen him twice since she left him in August 1980. Eventually he gave up and employed a variety of young women to run the shop.

Mohammed, then eight years old, and always his father's favourite, for a time visited him. "He used to give me money and ask me what my mother was doing. I didn't tell him, I just sat and listened. He was telling everyone Zana and Nadia were married and that they were happy.

"There were always women with him," he recalled. "One day I asked him why he had so many girlfriends — he was always taking them out at night when I arrived. He said some of the girls were for his men friends, and I would understand when I was older. I remember he used to sell qat to the Yemenis in the shop. They would all be chewing it."

Miriam, with a feeling of doom, wrote to the Foreign Office. As she had feared, the answer she received was unhelpful. The girls were dual nationals because their father was Yemeni. The Yemeni Government would consider that now they were in Yemen, and what is more married, they were Yemeni citizens. The only way her daughters would come home was if their husbands gave them permission to leave the country, thus enabling them to get exit visas. Miriam knew such an idea was hopeless — that Gohad Abdul Majid and Mohammed Abdul Khada would never allow it.

Nadia's social worker, Mary Birchell, who worked for the East Birmingham Family Service Unit, was, in Miriam's words, "fantastic". "She was very upset at what had happened," said Miriam. "Nadia was under her department's care, apart from anything else, so she was responsible for looking after her. She wrote to everyone — the Foreign Office, the British Embassy, lots of different charities, for me. She got the same response, though — everyone was sorry, but there was nothing they could do.

"Everyone told me to be patient, but I felt so depressed and desperate. It was very difficult. I lived on tranquillizers, and I lost loads of weight. People who see me now don't recognise me as the old Miriam."

The chief problem Miriam had, and her greatest torment, was that she did not know where her daughters were in Mokbana. She had a Post Office Box Number in Taiz, which Muthana had given her before the girls went on holiday. She wrote, but for months received no reply. She assumed the PO Box Number was false, and that therefore she had no means of communication with them, no way of knowing if they were alive or dead.

In desperation she visited Gohad at his home in Willows Road, Birmingham. Smugly, he told her that the marriages had taken place and there was nothing she could do about it, but he told her the names of the villages where her daughters were living — "Shubee" and "Hockail".

He insisted the the PO Box Number she had was genuine. She wrote another batch of letters to the girls, but again received no replies. She feared her daughters could have been moved to another part of the country and that she might never see them again.

On 23 October 1980, the British Embassy in Sana'a received a letter concerning the Muhsen sisters. It was from Nadia's social worker, Mary Birchell, writing on behalf of the East Birmingham Family Service Unit. The letter said that the sisters' mother was very concerned about her daughters. They had already been in the country for four months and the only news she had received from them had been two postcards when they had first arrived.

The British Consul now in Sana'a, Mr James Halley, who arrived in October 1987, commented: "The letter asked us to find out about the girls — whether they had been married, and what sort of state they were in. The trouble was all we had to go on concerning their whereabouts, was a PO Box Number in Taiz. We had no idea where the girls were."

It was the second communication the Embassy had had regarding the Muhsen sisters. On 7 August 1980, the British Embassy in Sana'a received a letter from one Zana Muhsen. In it she explained that she and her sister had recently arrived in Yemen and were now married. Now they wished to visit Britain, with their husbands, and would the Embassy please explain how they could set about doing so?

The British Consul saw no cause for concern in a straightforward request concerning visa applications for Yemeni men married to English women, which were not even followed up by a letter asking for a meeting. When the letter arrived in October, however, he passed it on to the Foreign Office, who in turn duly contacted Miriam, quoting the PO Box Number in Taiz. It turned out to be the same one that Miriam already had.

It was eight-year-old Mohammed who kept open the vital communication link between his sisters and Miriam. One day, after visiting the fish and chip shop, he brought home a pile of letters from his sisters. His father, he said, had been reading bits aloud to customers and some old Yemeni friends who were sitting in the shop. He told his mother and she asked him to bring them to her.

When his father's back was turned, Mohammed took them from his father's coat pocket. The first few, addressed to both Miriam and Muthana, said that the girls were happy, and loved Yemen, and their husbands, and the "kind men who brought us". But then there was a dramatic change. Zana wrote that she had been forced to write the previous letters by Mr Khada, who had been in the room with her, and who read them after she finished. This letter, she said, was telling the truth, and she had given it to a man in the village who had befriended her and Nadia. He had promised to take it to Taiz and get it safely posted, for, she warned, she suspected many of their letters were read by the agent, and never sent out of the country. She wrote: "Every night I cry. I am scared. Please don't make us suffer. Please, Dad, if you love us, you must let us come home to see you."

The letters were heartbreaking for Miriam to read — the more so because Zana and Nadia were assuming that she must have conspired with Muthana in selling them as brides. Naturally, because the girls did not know the truth, they also assumed their mother and father were still together.

Another read: "Mom, we are your daughters, please help us . . . you don't know what I have to go through . . . it's like slaving for them. Please let us come home . . . Mom, it does not seem as if we are your daughters any more because you are making us stay in this country . . .".

Although now in despair that the girls would ever receive her letters, Miriam wrote another batch to the PO Box Number in Taiz, telling the girls what had really happened, and promising to bring them home.

At first her letters got through, and the girls replied begging her to "do something quick". The letters were written on scraps of paper, half a page of an old exercise book, with writing all around the edges. Mrs Wellington, and her daughter, Lynette, Zana's best schoolfriend, also got a letter. In it, Zana wrote: "Tell Daddy to play the record, *Don't be cruel*, and please let us come home."

Then the girls' letters stopped. Later, it was discovered that a friend of Mr Khada and Mr Majid in Taiz was supposed to handle the PO Box mail. He was used to withholding certain letters if he chose to, and now on Gohad Majid's instructions, he was asked to stop both incoming and outgoing letters, unless he was told otherwise. Once this system was in practice very few letters got through.

Mrs Wellington remembers that in her letter from Zana, the girl asked for magazines and photographs. "We wrote coded messages in the magazines by underlining certain words," she recalled. "We even managed to smuggle photographs of the family inside and sent them off. But the girls never got them."

Mrs Wellington, who at the time ran a shop near Muthana's in Sparkbrook, vividly recalls how Muthana would proudly read out the "happy letters" to anyone he could get to listen. "I had got the truth in the letter from Zana, and also in the ones they had got to Miriam before their post was stopped," she said. "It used to make me sick, the way he went on. One day I met him in the street, and he started to get one out of his pocket. I just said to him: 'You pig. You sold your kids.' I felt like flattening him, there on the pavement. He looked ashamed and more or less ran off."

She said that her daughter, Lynette, nearly had a breakdown over what had happened to the sisters. "We were really worried about her, her father and I," she said. "She just used to sit and cry all the time for her friend, Zana. My husband, who is now dead, was very upset too. He couldn't understand how any father could sell off his kids like that."

Mrs Wellington said she feared at first that Miriam would end up in a mental hospital with a breakdown. "She was really in a terrible state. She was nearly out of her head with worry and the frustration of everything. She had always lived for her kids and she was like half her old self without them."

To try to help her friend, Mrs Wellington wrote to the Queen with the girls' story. She received a sympathetic reply back from a lady-in-waiting, with an address — that of Defence of Children International, based in Geneva. The letter said that this charity had in the past handled similar cases.

Both Miriam and Mrs Wellington wrote to the charity's chairman, Mr Nigel Cantwell. They each received a reply — that as the girls were dual nationals because they were married, there was little anyone could do. However, wrote Mr Cantwell, he had sought legal advice on one point concerning the marriages. As Miriam Ali and Muthana Muhsen had never been married,

بسم الله الرحمن الرحيم

حضر لدي الرجل الكامل العاقل مثنى احمد حسن قرية شقران
مريس يمن المقيم حالياً في المملكة المتحدة مدينة برمنجهام
بريطانيا وزوج إبنته ناديه مثنى احمد علي الراغبة فيه
محمد عبد الماجد نضر عبد الله من سكنة قرية الأشعوب مقبنه
المقيم حالياً في اليمن وقد تولى قبول عقد النكاح عن ولده
المذكور الرجل الكامل العاقل عبد الماجد نضر عبد الرحمن سكنة
قرية الأشعوب مقبنه المقيم حالياً في المملكة المتحدة مدينة برمنجهام
على المهر المتراضيين عليه الى ريال يمني كان هذا بحضور
الشهود وهم محمد ردمان سعيد حياش وعبد النور صالح سيف حقيل
وعبد الرحمن علي احمد صبر كلاهما من اليمن مقيمين حالياً في المملكة
المتحدة مدينة برمنجهام بتاريخ

٩ شعبان سنة ١٤٠٨ه الموافق ٢٢ يونيو ١٩٨٨م
كتب الحقير الى ربه الفقيه عبد الحافظ هزاع يزيد قرية الأشعوب
المقيم حالياً في المملكة المتحدة

التوقيع عبد الرحمن علي احمد سعيد مبركي
صالح محمد حاسب

Nadia's marriage document.

Miriam was legally their sole guardian. Her permission had not been sought on the marriages of her daughters, and therefore he considered the Yemeni Government might rule the marriages were illegal. He promised that he would write to the Yemeni Government and the British Embassy in Sana'a asking for information on the girls' welfare, and also seeking their opinion on the legality of the marriages.

Miriam was not much comforted. She knew the marriages were illegal, but — rightly as it turned out — did not have much hope that the Government of North Yemen would want to get involved in sorting out an irregular marriage. Also it gave her little satisfaction to think that Muthana could face criminal charges for what he had done. The only thing she wanted was to have her daughters home. She wrote to the Yemeni Government telling them that her daughters had been illegally married. She included the names of the villages and asked the authorities to investigate. She finally received a reply: the Government could find no trace of the villages in question on any of their maps.

Mrs Wellington then suggested that she should go to the Press, but Miriam was against it. "She was in a pitiful state," she recalls. "She said that someone — the Foreign Office, or Defence of Children — had strongly advised against media involvement in case the fathers in the villages got to hear about outside interest and moved the girls to an even more remote part of Yemen than that in which they were currently living.

"Apart from being an utter wreck over the girls, Miriam was also terrified that Muthana would try and take her other two daughters and do the same to them if he found out that she was not just going to forget about Zana and Nadia. Aisha and Tina were only 12 and ten years old, but they got scared too. They wouldn't see their father."

Early in December, Miriam heard that Muthana had received a tape-recording from the girls, saying how happy they were. On the tape, Zana is heard saying falteringly: "Daddy is a good man and Daddy loves us and when he comes here we will be very happy. We will be more happy than what you are in England. It's very, very, very lovely in the Yemen and when you come here, you will be very happy." She adds that the villagers had just killed a goat and they were all going to eat it for Christmas. Also on the tape are men's voices in Arabic. When we met her, Zana told us: "It broke my heart to make that tape, but I had to. Abdul Khada made me. He had spent a long time hitting me before I did it, and when I did, he was standing just behind me with Gohad."

Mohammed, on one of his "spying" visits to his father, saw the tape and pcoketed it. His mother played it at home. "It was terrible. I knew by the way Zana was talking that she was being forced," said Miriam. It was shortly after this that his father gave Mohammed an ultimatum. He had noticed that letters from the girls had gone from his coat. Mohammed said: "He called me over to him and said that I had to choose between him and my mother. If I stayed with my mother, he didn't want to see me any more. But if I chose him, then I could have whatever I wanted. I chose my mum. I knew what he had done and my mum needed me."

Chapter Four

Life in the villages of Mokbana ground on. After six months Nadia, who at school had been described as "slow", was fluent in Arabic, written and spoken. But she had become utterly withdrawn, never smiling.

Zana was at desperation point. Her husband's family seemed to hate her, no matter what she did to try to please them. The girls clung together, meeting in the fields or at the well to talk. Soon the families realised that so much talk meant less chores were done, and they suspected the girls were planning how they could escape.

"My mother-in-law really hated me," said Zana. "She used to tease me that I would never leave, and that I would die in the village, all black and shrivelled up like the old women. I wanted to die."

One day, when her mother-in-law was lying sick in the house, Zana went into her room, and took a bottle of pills from her table. She ran outside, down the track leading to the well, swallowing them as she went. "I wanted to go to sleep and never wake up," she said. "But my mother-in-law had seen me take the pills and had cried out to her older son, Mohammed. He came running after me and caught me. He made me choke, and I vomited them up. He was very sorry for me. He was a good man, but he was scared of his father, like they all are. He was very upset and said I must not do it again, and that he would try to help me if he could. I don't know why they stopped me, life was just as bad afterwards."

The families feared that both girls might commit suicide and so it was decided that Zana, the evil influence, should be taken away. Her father-in-law, Abdul Khada, took her to Campais, about 70 miles away. There, she virtually starved herself to death, so desperate was she to return to her sister. The villagers of Campais grew so frightened at the thought of a British girl dying in their midst, that a doctor was brought to her. Zana recalls: "He said I would die unless I went back to my sister because I told him I felt too sick to eat. Eventually I was taken back to Nadia."

A year passed, and then Nadia's father-in-law, Gohad Abdul Majid, returned to Birmingham. Miriam was unaware that he was again living in Sparkbrook. Occasionally her daughters' letters got through, each one more despairing than the last, begging her to rescue them. But in spite of the help of Mary Birchell, her friends and herself endlessly writing letters, and the intervention of Defence of Children International, Miriam found herself up against brick walls.

Mr Nigel Cantwell of Defence of Children International said that his organisation did the bulk of their work on the case between 1981 and 1982. "Basically there were a lot of leads that went astray. The first thing we did, through our mission here in Geneva was try to get the Yemeni authorities to investigate the girls' situation. After some considerable time, we got a letter back from them saying they had agreed to investigate. That letter is the only written proof we had that they knew about it. We wrote literally dozens of letters in '81 and '82, some got lost, some were never answered. We telephoned, and were told that everything was in hand. We waited for about a year for news and never got any further information from them, to this day.

"While we waited we tried to get background on Yemen from people who knew the country well, so we might be able to put together a picture for ourselves of the girls' situation. We were in touch with the British Consul in Sana'a, and again there, letters seem to have got lost because we had no joy with him.

"During 1983 we tried to get messages through to the girls via a traveller going to Yemen, but that was unsuccessful too. We were really at our wits' end with it by this time."

Still no one really knew where the girls were, except that it was very remote and they had no chance of independently travelling to Taiz, or even a larger village to get help. There were no detailed maps of Yemen available. The Foreign Office had expressed its concern, but repeated that they could not intervene because of the girls' dual nationality status.

Muthana, with a fresh supply of letters from Gohad, some of these now written in Arabic, was continuing to proclaim that the girls were happy and settled. Friends of Miriam's recall with what pleasure he boasted that his daughters could now write Arabic like native Yemenis.

In 1982, Miriam was the victim of a serious road accident. She was using a public telephone box, just round the corner from her home, when a car smashed into her, flattening the phone box and throwing her into the air. She had nearly lost her right eye, one knee-cap was shattered and one leg ripped by lacerations. A police car had seen the accident but failed to catch the driver. Her children had heard the crash and came running around the corner.

She was taken to hospital in Birmingham, where she underwent emergency surgery. After one week, she was frantic with worry about her children and discharged herself, in spite of her leg being encased in plaster. She went home and looked after her children, although she could not move, directing operations from a bed in her front room.

Towards the end of 1983, Zana's husband, Abdullah, now 16, visited England to have medical treatment for a heart condition. Mrs Wellington said that she remembered passing Muthana's shop and being called in by him. "He was standing in the shadows, very skinny and ill-looking," she said. "Gohad was there too, with the boy, and Muthana said: 'This is Zana's husband.' I said: 'Oh yes, and why isn't Zana with you?' I got no answer from any of them."

She told Miriam of the boy's presence, but Miriam did not go to see him. "It would have made me sick. Anyway, I might have had to talk to Muthana. I wasn't interested in the boy, all I wanted was my girls."

The boy overstayed his medical visa. The Home Office had issued a deportation notice, and were about to serve it on him when he returned to Yemen.

A month or so later, Nadia wrote to say that she was pregnant, but now, thankfully, her husband had gone to work in Saudi Arabia, as had Zana's husband and father-in-law. "At least now we will be left in peace," she wrote.

Again Miriam asked Mr Cantwell if she should approach the media to publicise the story, but he advised against it, except as a last resort. "We had always agreed with Miriam that to approach the Press could have negative repercussions on the girls," he said. "We feared that they could be moved and hidden, or even worse, because we were aware by this time that money was involved, in the form of bribes. That is why we now think the search party we thought we had organised for them never arrived. Our other fear was that we had to be relatively certain that the Yemeni authorities, if the story was made public, would not simply go on the defensive. They might refuse to co-operate in helping the girls, and say that their father had done nothing wrong in arranging their marriages — it was according to Yemeni customs. They might feel they were defending themselves against outside interference on a cultural basis."

More time passed: the British Embassy, according to its files on the case, record hearing nothing from between 19 April 1982 and February 1986. Miriam had not given up, she insists, she was merely doing as she was bid by the various agencies which were trying to help — waiting. During this period, on the suggestion of Mrs Wellington, she visited the surgery of Sparkbrook MP, Mr Roy Hattersley, the Shadow Home Secretary. She gave him letters from her daughters, and asked him to intervene. But she heard nothing more from him.

Miriam was also involved in a court action to claim compensation for her road accident. In 1984, Mr Cantwell records that he received a letter from her, telling him that if the money came through, she intended to visit her daughters, and bring them home herself. He wrote back, wishing her the best of luck, but adding that if her visit was unsuccessful he now thought she should publicise her daughters' plight. "It seemed the only alternative," he said. "If she failed, she would have to go to the Press — either through one journalist or by holding a press conference and inviting representatives of the Yemeni community."

The case for compensation was dragging on, and Miriam decided to settle out of court. She received £6,500 for her injuries, and was told that she could have got a lot more if she had persevered, but she had an urgent need for the money.

"Everyone was telling me to be patient, but I knew my daughters were going mad over there, and how could I keep asking them to stick it out and wait for God knows how many years more?" she said. "I had made my mind up I was going to get them."

She knew, through her daughters' smuggled letters, the names of their villages. Zana's brother-in-law, Mohammed, who had saved her when she took an overdose, was now living in Taiz with his wife and children and had promised to help Miriam visit the girls.

In February 1986, she wrote to the British Embassy requesting advice on how to get a visa for North Yemen. She was referred to the Embassy of the Yemen Arab Republic in Mayfair, London. Miriam, now agoraphobic, and terrified in particular of flying alone, decided to take her 13-year-old son, Mohammed, with her. She duly completed for herself and Mohammed the visa application forms, putting down the reason for her visit as "Mother, wishing to see her daughters". She sent off, as demanded, 1,000 dollars in traveller's cheques to prove she could provide for the trip, and enclosed £20 for the two visas.

Ten days later, their visas arrived. Mrs Wellington remembers she was amazed at the courage and determination her friend was now displaying. "She had always seemed dazed, and not quite with it," she said. "A sorrowful little thing, to be pitied. Now she was like a lion."

On 2 April, the British Vice-Consul in Yemen, Mr Colin Page, was sitting in his office when guests were announced, and shown in. Before him stood a small, bedraggled woman, and her young son. The woman, Miss Miriam Ali, said she had come to take her daughters home — Zana and Nadia Muhsen, who had been kidnapped and were living in Mokbana.

Mr Page was extremely unhelpful, said Miriam — and her opinion was backed up by a host of British expatriates living in Yemen. "He told me I was wasting my time," she recalled. "He was very rude, hostile even. He said that I didn't have a hope. That because the girls did not have their passports, new ones would have to be issued, and even then it was impossible for them to get out. He said that they were considered to be dual nationals, because of their father and the fact they were now living in Yemen.

"The only way they could leave was to get permission from their husbands, and then the Yemeni authorities would issue them with exit visas. He said that he did not even know where they were. I told him the names of the villages, but he said that was no good, because there were no detailed maps of Mokbana.

"He said I shouldn't even bother trying to get to the girls, and that I should go home and forget about them. I was amazed at his attitude. We had travelled such a long way, and we were so tired, and he didn't even offer us a glass of water. As we were going out of the door, he said: 'I should watch your son, if I were you. They would like to get their hands on him, too, I shouldn't wonder.'

"That was the great British Embassy that everyone was relying on to get my girls home. I was so disappointed I could hardly speak. I had thought they would help, perhaps travel with us, and get us into the villages. I thought if I was actually there, they could help with the exit visas and make the Yemeni Government do something to help. But he just didn't want to know."

The next morning, Miriam and Mohammed travelled to Taiz by bus. Zana, in her last letter, had told her mother that there was a hotel in the town, opposite the Post Office. She advised her mother to stay there, and ask for the postal agent, Nasser Saleh. Zana thought he might help. If that failed, Mohammed ran a chemist's shop in Taiz, Zana said. She had enclosed a muzzy photograph of him, which Miriam carried.

She had no joy at the Post Office, so with the photograph in her hand, she and Mohammed trailed around Taiz for three days, asking anyone who understood English if they recognised the man. Eventually, somebody did, and they were taken to his house. "He was all right," said Miriam. "He said he would take us to the villages but first he would have to arrange a jeep.

"We went back next morning, and he said he had to telephone his father — Zana's father-in-law — where he worked in Saudi Arabia. He looked scared, even though he was a grown man, with kids of his own. Anyway, he phoned, and I heard him say 'Miriam' — he must have been telling him that I was there.

"Then he said his father wanted to talk to me. I took the phone and that man Abdul Khada said: 'Hullo, I hope you haven't come to cause trouble.' I said something like, 'What do you mean? I have come to see my daughters.' He said: 'Because if you have

come to cause trouble, I've got the girls' father's consent to take
them to Marais in Aden. I'll just take them there and wipe my
hands clean.' I didn't know what he was talking about, but it was
probably true they had got some sort of letter from Muthana in
case of trouble. He sounded threatening, but scared at the same
time, like he knew he had done wrong. I just said I had come to
see if my daughters were all right, not to cause trouble — but I
was going to get them back to England soon.

"His son talked to him more, then he said it was OK, and we
would go to the villages. Then suddenly he looked very ashamed
and told us that his father and Gohad had bought the girls from
Muthana. It was the first time my suspicions were confirmed."

Miriam remembers the journey as an awful nightmare trek
through a mountain desert, with the only signs of life being some
goats and a few children tending them. Mohammed said: "It was
like a bomb had hit the place. There was nothing there; it was so
dry, with little mud houses on the mountains."

The reunion with her daughters was, as might be expected,
extremely emotional. The girls were convinced she had come to
take them home, but Miriam had to tell them things had not
worked out as she had hoped.

She found that both her daughters were pregnant, Zana
expecting her first child in May, and Nadia about a month
afterwards. She met her grandson, two-year-old Haney, who at
first was too frightened of strangers to come near her.
Fortunately, neither the husbands nor fathers-in-law were
present. They had not been home for six months.

She and Mohammed spent two weeks with the girls, staying
first at one village, then at the other. She was horrified at the way
in which they were living and the back-breaking work they had to
do. Zana told her that one day Abdul Khada, her father-in-law,
had forced her to make twenty trips down the mountain to the
well to fetch water. When she had finished, he kicked her down
the stairs for not also having gone to a neighbouring village to buy
food. Miriam found that there was scarcely any food to eat, and
after her first week hired a jeep to go into Taiz to buy provisions.

Her daughters clung to her like limpets, begging her to take
them home, although finally they accepted that they would have
to wait.

The family were seldom allowed to be on their own. Apparently Abdul Khada had sent word with his son that the girls and their mother were to be spied on by the villagers, several of whom spoke English. Whenever they thought they had crept away to talk, they would find an old man who understood English had come to sit on a nearby rock.

They told her their story, filling in many missing gaps. Both their fathers-in-law had told them they had been sold by their father for £1,300 each — there was no doubt. They identified a man living in Birmingham who had organised the marriage and provided the certificates — it was essential, they said, that their mother find him and expose him. Miriam heard how her daughters had been forced into bed with their husbands, and about Zana's suicide bid.

Her daughters told her that they were so terrified of being punished, that they did exactly what they were told — which included never leaving the villages. Miriam was particularly concerned for Nadia, who was having to look after her mother-in-law's young children, a boy and girl. Their mother, apparently, had gone to Birmingham to be with Gohad eight months previously, promising it was only going to be a three-month stay. Heavily pregnant, and with a toddler in tow already, Nadia had to care for the children because no one else would in her village of Ashube.

To try to comfort the girls, Miriam told them about all the different people at home who were trying to help. She showed them letters she had received from Mr Cantwell and asked them to write letters to him, telling what they had been through. She heard her daughters curse their father, and joined in. She told them of the suffering she had endured being separated from them, and how Muthana had taunted her and lied. Touchingly, the girls begged her to keep their younger sisters away from him, in case the same fate should befall them.

Miriam said: "They were so good, so patient. They kept telling me not to worry, that they would wait until someone came. They were so brave. It broke my heart. I felt so useless."

Some of the village women were kind, she remembers. "One woman came from right over the other side of the mountain to see me. She sat down on the ground and cried and said it was so wrong what had happened, and that the girls must go home with their mother. She, and lots of the other women, couldn't believe that I had come all this way to see them and then had to leave them behind. They were good people, but they were only village women and there was nothing they could do."

Miriam could have stayed longer than two weeks, but although she and her daughters both wanted her and Mohammed to stay forever, they knew she was powerless in Yemen.

"Zana said to me: 'Go home, Mum, with our letters for Mr Cantwell, and let him do everything officially. We will wait.' I told them that as soon as I got back, I was going to get a telephone installed and phone up Mr Cantwell in Geneva, and tell him everything, and that it wouldn't be long after that before people came for them.

"They were terribly worried that if people did come, the police in Taiz would get to know about it. You see, they told me that they had heard that twice before people had come looking. I don't know if it was through Mr Cantwell's charity or the Red Cross. But on both occasions they had relied on the police — and the police had been bribed not to do anything. The police got 2,000 rials — about £200 — on both occasions. I had not realised the place was so corrupt.

"The girls were crying when they said it was better I go home quickly, so I could get everything organised. I tried not to cry, but Mohammed was very upset. He loved his sisters, and he hated his father so much for what he had done that he said as soon as he was big enough he was going to kill him. He was only a little boy, really, but he understood everything, and he was very bitter against his dad."

Before Miriam left, Zana said that she had a tape recorder, and that she would make a tape for Mr Cantwell, as well as the letters she and Nadia had already written. Miriam could not bear to hear it — and to this day has never listened to her daughter telling her story. Zana went on to the flat roof of her house to record it.

Just before Miriam and Mohammed left, there came news that Zana's father-in-law was on his way to the villages from Saudi Arabia, to sort out any trouble Miriam may be causing. The girls urged their mother to leave immediately, saying he would probably never arrive, but that it would be better if she was not there. Later, they disclosed they were terrified at the prospect of what Abdul Khada might do to them if the villagers reported their plans to return home. But, fortunately, he did not come to the villages.

A letter from Muthana telling the authorities not to allow the girls home.

Chapter Five

A girl's voice crying: "I want to get out of here as soon as possible. Mr Cantwell, if only you could see how we are living. It is terrible. I've been suffering for six years and there's nothing I could have done about it anyway, 'cos I'm stuck in the village and I've got nobody to turn to, but when my mum told me about you, that you are trying to help us, I was very happy of the thought that somebody cares.

"I, I, I've never heard anything about it, I dunno, it's just terrible. They're keeping us here against our will and I dunno what for. I just wanna go home to my mother . . .

" . . . I hope and pray to God today that when my mum gets back and she lets you know everything, I hope they come for us and just take us. I don't wanna stay, I don't wanna stay here, I'm going to go crazy. Honestly, I'll kill myself, even, if I have to. I'd rather die than live here. Yes, Mr Cantwell, it is THAT BAD. It is more, it is more worser than what anyone would ever think. I don't think no girl's been through what we've been through. And they forced me to go to bed with him and I said NO. They said, 'You'd better because if you don't, we'll hold you down,' so I had to. (*Crying*). What do you think about that, Mr Cantwell?"

Mr Cantwell, sitting in his office in Geneva, thought it one of the most heart-rending stories he had ever heard. Zana, speaking in her Birmingham accent, telling how she and her sister were living, hearing their pleas for rescue all directed towards him. Zana, sounding suddenly ashamed, saying: " . . . the one I am supposed to be married to, I hate him. I cannot, I cannot accept him, I just don't want him, but it happened. See, I'm due to have a baby in about a month's time, and my sister, she's already got a baby son, he's two years old." Then the voice is angry, defiant:

"Well, they don't belong to us, anyway, 'cos we was forced."

Completely breaking down when she speaks of her father: "I don't even know him, I hate him. (*Crying*). He was so wicked, and he don't care. I used to write him letters, and tell him, 'Dad, please let me come home,' but he doesn't answer me. (*Crying*).

"I can't accept him as a father, ever, ever again. I'll never, ever forgive him all his life, and I'll curse his grave."

She begs Mr Cantwell to send in reporters to rescue them, but warns that two previous attempts to reach them have been stopped by bribery — presumably the two occasions when Mr Cantwell had asked the Yemeni authorities to trace the girls, and the traveller. "When your reporters get through, I hope, and they take us for questioning, or anything, they are going to try and make excuses. They are going to say, 'Zana made a tape for her mum and dad that she's happy,' and they'll let them listen to it, you know, to make them believe that I said it. But I was forced to, Mr Cantwell, you must believe me.

". . . he (*her husband*) is going to try to make excuses to the Government. He's going to say, 'I buy her jewellery and gold and I give her clothes, and everything.' Mr Cantwell, my mother is my gold, I only want my mum.

"I don't even wear their gold . . . don't want it, don't want nothing. It's just hard work, and that's all we've been through, hard work in the village. I had blisters on my hands and feet from working in the hot weather. I just don't know how to explain it. It's just terrible. I get a headache just thinking about it.

"And now my mum, she has to leave us again. (*Crying*). My heart's going to rip to pieces when she goes. (*Crying*). I thought we was going to go with her, as she said, but it didn't turn out right. (*Crying*). I have faith in you, Mr Cantwell, and I have faith in God and I'll be patient."

Miriam had sent the tape and letters to Mr Cantwell on 2 May, a day after she got back from Yemen. "We started everything rolling again," he said. "The tape was a cry from the heart, extremely moving." The charity wrote again to the Yemeni Government; again no response.

However, they had recently opened a London office, and their representative, barrister Geraldine Van Bueren, got in touch with Miriam. Miriam travelled to London to see her a couple of times, but never really felt at ease with her. "She said to me, 'Why don't the girls just get on a bus, and go into Taiz?' and I had explained to her dozens of times about how remote and dangerous the area they were in was, and how anyway they were so scared of the men in the village, they obeyed them and never set foot outside the villages unless they were escorted."

However, Ms Van Bueren did all she could to help, like many others before her. She organised meetings with leading Muslims in London to seek their expertise on how Muslim marriages were arranged. She made contact with members of the Foreign Office and tried to push them into acting. But in the eyes of the Foreign Office, she was barking up the wrong tree.

The British Embassy in Sana'a have in their file a letter from Ms Van Bueren, dated 13 August 1986. It states that in her opinion, having done a great deal of research, Miriam's daughters were not actually dual nationals, because they had been married without their knowledge, and against their will. Mr James Halley, the Consul to North Yemen since late 1987, commented: "The girls are not dual nationals because of their marriage, whether it be a true or false one. Their Yemeni nationality comes from their father, and was strengthened when they were brought here. They are now considered Yemeni citizens. I am afraid Ms Van Bueren was on the wrong track."

Miriam decided to at least try to get her daughters new passports. That way, she thought, they might be able to escape from their villages and use them to get home. Early in January 1987, Miriam wrote to the Embassy requesting they send her application forms for the passports, which, a month later, they did.

She realised that she had no recent photographs of the girls that would be considered suitable for the passports, so in March she wrote to her daughters, asking if they could travel to Taiz to get photographs. In April, she received a despairing reply: "Mom, you know we're in a prison, and you asked us to go to Taiz for the photos. If you would have asked me to climb Mount Everest barefooted it would have been a lot easier. How on earth can we get to Taiz? Every time I read your line where you said, 'You have to get the photos', it stabs me like a knife, because we can't, we're stuck here in this goddamn village. I knew that something would go wrong, I had the feeling all the way, and I hate myself.

"What we gonna do now, ROT HERE? Can't Geraldine (Van Bueren) or Cantwell do something? Phone him and explain to him, that we haven't got any small recent photos. We have got a Kodak film, and we took two each and I cut them like passport photos, but I've got that feeling that they won't do any good."

The lack of photographs seemed another insurmountable barrier. However, Miriam completed the passport forms and sent them with old pictures of her daughters to the Embassy. She enclosed 600 rials, as requested, but heard no more word from the Embassy. Now she felt she was back to square one. With her friend, Anne Sufi, she visited Gohad Abdul Majid's house in Willows Road. There the two women found Muthana talking with his friend. He was immediately on the defensive and Miriam on the attack. She accused him again of selling the girls, and again he denied it. Miriam begged Gohad to allow the girls home on a holiday — he refused. He said: "They are not your daughters any more, they are mine." Mrs Sufi said: "I said to Gohad that Miriam was going to get the girls back, and if they would not help, we would do it another way. He said: 'What other way?' I meant go to the newspapers, but I didn't tell him. I said again that the girls were going to come home, and he laughed in my face. He said: 'Give me the money, and I will go over to Mokbana myself and bring the girls home.' He said that Miriam would never do anything, that she had forgotten about the first two children being taken, and that she would forget about Zana and Nadia."

But in spite of the fighting words, Miriam was just about finished. Her daughters, in their letters, were now screaming for help. One from Zana read: " . . . what on earth is going on, why so long . . . Mom, for God's sake do something, I'm going crazy." Mrs Sufi suggested Miriam should talk to a priest whom she knew, Father John.

The priest had ideas about hiring some sort of "A-Team" to go in and kidnap the girls. He said he knew some men who might be able to arrange it. But again, after a time, nothing more was heard.

The only good news during this bleak period was the arrival of a letter from the girls telling their mother that their brother,

Ahmed, had found them. A soldier in the army, he had been on leave in his home village of Marais, South Yemen, when an old man who had just returned after living in Birmingham told him of his sisters. He had visited them immediately and promised to do all he could to help. Miriam said: "I broke down when I heard that Ahmed was alive and knew about the girls. It was the first I had heard of him in over twenty years. I told the girls in my letters what had happened to him and Leila and that made them hate their father even more." For a brief spell, Miriam hoped that Ahmed, as a soldier, might have been able to rescue the girls. But he was recalled to his duties back in the south.

Then Miriam heard about a man, living nearby, who helped people — at a price. He was Mr Alf Dickens, who ran his own business, called Phoenix Enterprise. He had previously been a community worker in the Handsworth area after the riots in 1985. He decided to set up in business, as the United Kingdom's first Community Consultant. For £5 a day, he helped people sort out their lives. Miriam talked over with Mrs Sufi the prospect of approaching Mr Dickens for help and they both thought: "Well, what have we got to lose?"

It was in September 1987 when Miriam first visited Mr Dickens, a sprucely turned-out, neat man in middle age, who sported a moustache and, always, a bow-tie. He listened to the story, and the tape, when Miriam was out of the room. He wanted to help, but was stumped.

One evening he was drinking in a pub when he spotted a journalist he knew, who worked for the *Birmingham Post*. He told him Miriam's story. The journalist happened to be the news editor of the paper and the next day he asked one of his feature writers, Tom Quirke, to look into the story further.

Through Alf Dickens, Mr Quirke met Miriam, heard the story, listened to the tape and read the girls' letters. He later told Mrs Sufi: "It was the biggest story the *Birmingham Post* ever had." He spent over a week talking to Miriam, getting her to retell the story again and again. "We needed to be absolutely sure it was genuine," he said.

He visited Muthana and got little out of him except that he had been unhappy with the girls' behaviour and was keen for them to learn from the Yemen's traditional Muslim culture. Muthana told Mr Quirke: "I said that if they didn't like it they should write to me and they could come home."

Although both Miriam and Zana on the tape-recording accused Muthana of selling brides, the *Birmingham Post*'s lawyers were "extremely wary" of any such claim being put in the newspaper. So when the first story appeared on the front page on 27 November 1987 it said that two Birmingham sisters had disappeared under mysterious circumstances.

Alf Dickens, who had by this time, according to Miriam, virtually taken over her life, wanted to know the next step in getting wider publicity. Mr Quirke suggested that he hold a press conference. This was duly done on 27 November, the same day that the *Birmingham Post* ran its first story.

Miriam did not think much of the press conference. "I have never been good at meeting people, and in that front room of Alf's, with all those journalists, I felt terrified. I got the feeling lots of them didn't believe me. And Alf was beginning to worry me. He had said he wanted to help me, but when I asked him about having to pay him money for all the days' work, he didn't say anything.

"Then, with some of the journalists he kept going on about how much this case was costing him, and how if a newspaper would only pay his fare, and expenses, and mine too, because I knew how to get to the girls, he would go there and get them back. He made me feel that I couldn't talk for myself, and that he was in control. He even kept saying 'our kids', as if they were his daughters. But I thought that even if I didn't like the way he was going about things, it was worth sticking with him if he could do anything."

On the Friday night Tom Quirke contacted *The Observer* with the story. I had been working on a story about caravans and had just realised it had little chance of making that week's paper, or to be honest, any week's paper. My news editor, Angela Gordon, came over with a copy of the *Birmingham Post*, and told me to have a look at the story on missing children. On reading it through, and particularly the father's quotes, it seemed as if a large chunk of it was missing — that the father was far more involved, indeed he must be responsible for the girls' marriages.

I telephoned Alf Dickens of Phoenix Enterprise on his

24-hour number in Birmingham. He was more than prepared, he told me, to "get the mother round" in the morning, and help her tell the story. I also spoke to Mr Roy Hattersley's office who confirmed that he, the MP for the mother's constituency, had written to Home Secretary Douglas Hurd asking him to intervene. The Foreign Office confirmed that a "local agent" in a town near where the girls were living had been despatched to the girls to find out whether they were being held against their will.

At eight o'clock the following morning, *Observer* photographer John Riordan and I were in his car, belting up the M1. We had only until noon to get the story and pictures in the paper for Sunday's edition. Luckily John had lived in Birmingham and knew the road, Heathfield Road in Handsworth, where Alf Dickens lived. It was also his office.

Mr Dickens, who immediately struck me as a sort of "Arthur Daley" type in a bow-tie, answered the door. The mother was not there, he said, but he would get her in about an hour. Time was too short for us to wait, it was then nearing ten o'clock. Mr Dickens, a voluble man, told us that the father of the girls had sold them — for £1,300 each. The mother had evidence of it on a tape from one of the girls, and if we had half an hour, he could play it to us. We didn't have half an hour. I decided that while the mother was on her way, we would go and talk to the father. Mr Dickens advised us that Tom Quirke had already done so, and he would be able to introduce us to him. "He is not a nice man," he said. I telephoned Tom Quirke at home, and he arranged to meet us in 15 minutes outside a fish and chip shop at 166 Stratford Road, Sparkbrook.

We got to the shop with five minutes to spare. Mr Quirke arrived and we then had the problem of raising Mr Muhsen. The rundown shop was shut and showed no signs of opening. Mr Quirke told us that Mr Muhsen had a flat above the shop, and often left it at around 10.30 a.m. It was approaching that, but the closed curtains above the shop front showed no sign of moving. With time pressing, we decided we would have to wake him up.

Beside the shop was an alleyway, leading to the back of the premises. We trooped around. It was very derelict, piles of rubbish, broken furniture, bits of corrugated iron lying strewn about. There was a heavy metal door at the back of number 166.

We hammered on this. No response. I picked up a brick and banged on the door. Still no response. We all began shouting. John left to go to the front of the shop to see if there was any life there.

Suddenly a head poked out of an upstairs window — Mr Muhsen, fresh from his bed. Mr Quirke called up to him, that he had some people who wished to talk to him. "Ten minutes," yelled Mr Muhsen.

Back we went to the front, a little concerned that Mr Muhsen would not appear at the appointed time. The shop had just been opened by a Greek man, who now ran it, paying money to Mr Muhsen which in turn he paid the mortgage with. The surly manager was not at all pleased when we came in and walked to the back where the stairs led to the upstairs flat. We waited, then from round the corner at the bottom of the stairs came Mr Muhsen's head. "Yes?" he said.

Mr Quirke had produced a tape-recorder and pressed the record button. I went over and shook hands with Mr Muhsen, saying I was from *The Observer* and wished to talk to him. Mr Muhsen did not seem too keen, in fact he started edging away.

He was of average height, skinny and unshaven with heavy bags under his eyes. "Mr Muhsen, I want to talk to you about your daughters," I said.

"Everybody wants to talk to me about my daughters," he said.

At this juncture, the Greek manager, now clad in a greasy overall, intervened. He lumbered over to me and started rubbing his fingers together: "Money," he said. "Money before he talks to you." I said there would be no money. Mr Muhsen was trying to nip upstairs again, so, seeing my quarry escaping, I called: "Mr Muhsen, did you sell your daughters?"

The effect was electric. The man seemed almost to be choking with rage. He turned back and shoved me, then he screamed: "You prove it, you prove I got money for my daughters, and I cut my throat." With a dramatic gesture, which John caught on film, he made a slicing motion across his throat.

Mr Quirke intervened, trying to calm the situation. Mr Muhsen was still gibbering with rage, but he sat down at a table in the shop. Again I asked him about his daughters. This time, he admitted that he knew about the marriages. He admitted sending them as brides to Yemen, when they thought they were going on a

Muthana Muhsen, the father of Nadia and Zana, November 1987.

six-week holiday. He explained: "I did not want them to grow up in Birmingham where they would marry a black or they would become prostitutes, like their mother. In Yemen, they are good. They are Muslim. No one does anything bad to them. What they say is untrue, they are happy. Everyone says they are not, but they are. I have letters that say they are happy."

I looked at one of the letters later. It read: "Daddy, if you love us please let us come home."

Mr Muhsen got to his feet and said he was going to have a cup of tea and his breakfast. Again, he reiterated, with a vivid demonstration, the throat-cutting threat if we could prove he had sold his girls.

We did not have any more time; we thanked him for talking to us, and left. Mr Quirke seemed excited and asked if his newspaper could have the photograph John had taken of the slitting of the throat. We said we would talk about it later, we had to get back and see the mother.

Ben Gibson, April 1987.

Chapter Six

Miriam Ali, a tiny, dark-haired woman, was sitting on a sofa in the front-room which served as Mr Dickens' office. A few photographs of her daughters in Arab dress lay beside her — pictures she had taken on her visit the previous year. She was chain-smoking and seemed extremely nervous. Because time was so short, John took her outside to be photographed, then left for London.

With much prompting from Mr Dickens and Mr Quirke, she told her story. Mr Dickens said that they needed money from a newspaper to finance a trip for himself and Miriam to get the girls. Miriam said: "All the men in the village are armed, but if we went at the right time, they might all be away working in Saudi Arabia."

Alf then outlined his plan: "If your paper can pay us the money, I'll buy a gun in Sana'a. These men in the village, if they are there when we get there, won't do anything when they see I am armed. We can go in, no discussions, just get the girls and their kids in the jeep, and we will be off before anyone has noticed.

"We will take them to Sana'a, to the British Embassy who've sat round doing nothing for seven years, and we will stay there until they issue exit visas for the girls. They will be so embarrassed that they will have to do it. We will just sit it out. And whichever newspaper pays, gets the exclusive story."

I asked if there was a telephone I could use to file my story to *The Observer*, and he showed me into another room, from which I made a transfer charge call. Afterwards Mr Dickens reappeared and told me that really Miriam was not capable of going out to Yemen on her own to bring her girls back. "I have to tell her everything," he said. "What to say, who to talk to. She is really a nervous wreck. She wouldn't be able to go out there without me. She needs me to be with her."

We went back into the other room, where Miriam by now was reading that morning's national newspapers, a few of which had run the story, under such headlines as "Sex slave sisters sold in Yemen". Miriam was very unhappy. "They have missed out everything important," she said. "All they have done is write about the girls being forced to sleep with the boys."

Mr Dickens decided that I should hear the tape from Zana. "Go out of the room, Miriam, go next door," he said, and she obeyed. "She can't bear to hear it," he explained. I heard the tape, took a copy of it, and left.

On Sunday morning, *The Observer* ran the story, "British girls sold as Yemen brides", saying that Mr Muhsen had admitted sending the girls as brides. The following Wednesday Mr Muhsen surrendered to some extent. Now being harangued by the Press every time he set foot outside his fish and chip shop, he admitted on tape to Mr Quirke that his daughters had been unaware of the marriages, as had their mother. He said: "I showed my girls photographs of the two boys. We hoped that when they got to Yemen the girls would get on well with the boys and want to marry them. In the Yemen men and women are not allowed to walk down the street together if they are not married, let alone touch each other. . . . But I insisted that if the girls did not want to marry the boys, then that was that and the certificates must be returned to me."

He admitted that Miriam had been entirely unaware of the marriages, although he was later to deny this statement, and in fact changed his story almost daily from this point. Reporters from many national newspapers, but in particular the *Sunday Mirror*, who had also run a story the previous Sunday, were now virtually camping outside his house, and that of Mr Gohad Abdul Majid in Willows Road. Mr Majid called the police and complained of harassment. The reporters were asked to leave.

That week I tried to find out whether the "local agent" sent by the British Embassy had managed to discover anything about the sisters. I was told by the Foreign Office that unfortunately the information given by the mother on her daughters' whereabouts was unclear. The agent, a British man working in Taiz, had told the Embassy that the area known as Mokbana was "very remote" — too remote to set off looking for two British girls. But there had been an attempt by the Embassy to get a meeting arranged with the Ministry of Foreign Affairs. The first attempt had failed, but another was going to be made. The Embassy's legal adviser was also working on the complicated issue of whether the girls were Yemeni citizens.

A fiery Ms Van Bueren, from Defence of Children International, said that the legal investigation was merely a "red herring". She said: "I feel the Foreign Office is just trying to find ways of passing the buck. The nationality issue is clear — the girls were forced into marriage with Yemenis, and are therefore still British citizens. They are clearly extremely unhappy and should be brought home by the Foreign Office. It is incredible, don't you agree, that when Miss Ali went to see the Vice Consul, he was not interested in her story that her daughters, two British citizens, were held as prisoners in Yemen?"

Ms Van Bueren also claimed that the Muhsen sisters were not the only girls sold as brides by their families. She said that when she first contacted the Foreign Office on Miss Ali's behalf, to ask about the British girls who had been duped into marriage, the response had been: "Which ones?"

On the following Sunday, *The Observer* ran another story that there were more "child brides" from England taken to Yemen, and currently living there as married women, no one knowing whether they were happy or not.

Ms Van Bueren had also expressed the concern of Defence of Children International about the sort of publicity the case was getting, and confirmed that they had been reluctant for Miriam to approach the Press. They were particularly concerned that she was now "in tow" with someone who charged for helping people.

Mr Dickens, who was by this time phoning me almost daily to see whether the newspaper would pay for his trip, said that he would not be charging Miriam for the work he was doing on her behalf. He was doing his utmost to get a decision from us, and claimed that all sorts of other papers were looking at the funding of the operation. The *Sunday Mirror* was one.

The Observer was looking at the possibility at this time of sending a reporter and photographer to Yemen to find the girls, but considered a gung-ho rescue bid by Mr Dickens would be extremely dangerous, not just for journalists, but for the girls and their mother. Mr Dickens was becoming rather aggressive; he repeated that if we did not agree to foot the bill, many others were prepared to. He was refusing at this stage to give me the mother's telephone number — he said that she could not cope with journalists directly, but only through him.

During the second week of December 1987, I had a telephone call from the *Sunday Mirror*. They wanted to know what we were doing, and whether we were intending to "send" on the story. It seemed to be the next logical step, but it still had not been finally decided whether the story was worth the risks it would involve, or whether it would be even possible to find the girls. The instructions that Miriam, through Mr Dickens, had given us were scant, to say the least: "Drive out of Taiz on the road — there is only one — and then after about half an hour turn right. The villages are about two and a half hours into the mountains."

The *Sunday Mirror* said they were not prepared simply to visit the sisters — if they went it was to bring them home. *The Observer* felt that Mr Dickens would be more of a hindrance than a help, and that his leaning towards a shoot-out among bandits was potentially deadly. As the mother would not go without him, it was decided *The Observer* should go alone.

I contacted the Foreign Office about the availability of visas for the Yemen Arab Republic. They said it could take journalists up to three months to be granted a visa. This was confirmed by a woman from the Embassy of the Yemen Arab Republic. "Yes, journalists of course can come to the Yemen," she said on the telephone. "First they must write to us with the reasons why, and then this letter is sent to the Ministry of Foreign Affairs in Sana'a who decide whether to grant the visa."

We had a strong suspicion that once we gave the reason for our visit to Yemen, the visa application might be unsuccessful. Also three months was too long to wait. It was thought it might be best to send a journalist working out of Cairo into North Yemen, because at the time oil had been discovered and was about to be pumped into an offshore tanker for the first time. Apparently journalists in Cairo were being issued with visas for the purpose of reporting on the country's oil. But it would have been difficult for a journalist on an organised tour of oil-wells to have slipped off on his own expedition to Mokbana to discover the Muhsen sisters.

On Wednesday, 9 December, photographer Ben Gibson, who had taken an interest in the story and had found out about flights, and I were told to have a go at getting visas — as tourists. We were informed by Thomas Cook's that it could take ten days, but a friendly Cook's operator told us that if we turned up at the Embassy with completed visa application forms, 500 dollars each in cash or traveller's cheques, return air-tickets and passport-sized photographs we might be able to get them in 24 hours. He said that he had a contact at the Embassy whom he would try to talk to in order to ease the issuing of the visas. We did not tell him we were journalists, just in case he felt duty-bound to relay the information to his contact.

Ben and I came up with a cover-story about why we should wish to visit Yemen just before Christmas. It wasn't a very good one. We knew that a Muslim country would take a dim view of boyfriends and girlfriends, and that the woman in particular would be open to all sorts of criticism. Marriage, even for the sake of the story, was out of the question, so we were engaged (I had actually just got engaged, so there was a ring to prove it). We wouldn't be able to go on a honeymoon, because of Ben's work as an artist. This was the only time-off available to us, and unless we were able to fly out on Friday 12 December, we would lose the only holiday we could have. The reason it was such short notice was that I, a typist, had only just been told I could have the next seven days off.

We turned up at Thomas Cook's the next morning at 8.30 a.m., just after it opened. The friendly tour operator was extremely sympathetic when we poured out our story, and offered to supply us with dummy air-tickets to speed things up. These were valid tickets, which would prove to the Embassy we were booked for the flight on Friday afternoon on Yemenia Airways. We could hand them in with our applications, but we had to return them before we travelled using our own tickets. With our visa forms completed, and having drawn the dollars, we jumped into a taxi for South Street, Mayfair.

The Embassy was not, as we had feared, surrounded by other journalists impersonating tourists: the Consular Department, down a flight of narrow stone steps leading to the basement, was empty. Behind a glass window we glimpsed a man drinking tea.

He reluctantly rose and took our forms, tickets and dollars. I don't think he was terribly interested in our story, or maybe he just did not understand English. "Tourists?" he asked, then told us to come back the following afternoon. We explained our flight was at 4.30 p.m., so he said: "Tomorrow at 2 p.m.". If that had really been our flight time, we would have protested more, but as it was at 6 p.m., we smiled our thanks.

That night I managed to get hold of Miriam through a series of phone calls, starting with Ms Van Bueren. I had decided to deal with Miriam direct, rather than through Mr Dickens. She was delighted to hear that we were going, but desperate that we bring the girls home. I explained that we would do what we could, but she knew better than us about the dangers that could entail.

The message she had for her daughters was that she loved them, she said. In spite of the fact that she kept breaking down, she was surprisingly practical, considering that Mr Dickens had implied she was scarcely capable of stringing two words together without his support. She told me that a schoolfriend of her daughters had been in contact, having received the most recent letter, dated 8 November, from Zana. In it, she appeared to be almost giving up hope of returning home. She wrote: "I don't know whether I'll be coming out of here or not. All I know is that my Mom is trying her best. It's a prison here, just looking at hills and valleys everywhere through barred windows. I don't go nowhere. I have grown to hate myself."

Miriam told me that when we got to Taiz, we should try to meet up with Mohammed Abdul Khada, Zana's brother-in-law, who had helped her reach the girls the year before. She said he lived opposite the Ganad Hotel in the town.

Mr Roy Hattersley, who many years before had been approached by Miriam for help, had now met her again and promised he would do everything he could to get her daughters home. He had written to the Foreign Secretary, Sir Geoffrey Howe, condemning the Foreign Office for its handling of the Muhsen case. He wrote: "I do not accept the argument that the Foreign Office is powerless to assist Miss Ali, the girls' mother, because the girls have Yemeni citizenship.

"Mr Muhsen, the father, was previously a citizen of the colony of Aden, and came to this country on a colonies passport."

"He was still a colonial citizen when the girls were born. The girls could only have acquired Yemeni citizenship through marriage if a marriage ceremony had taken place.

"This is not the case and even the father has now admitted that he simply gave the girls away in marriage without any kind of ceremony.

"The Foreign and Commonwealth Office have, all along, taken the attitude that they cannot interfere simply because these girls have a Yemeni father. No attempt has been made to investigate the validity of the marriage and the circumstances under which these girls were taken to Yemen. I find this totally unacceptable.

"These girls should be brought home and brought home soon. They are British and they do not want to be in Yemen. They were taken there and married through deceit and force. Last week your office complained to mine about lack of facts. I have now provided the facts. And, having heard the tape recording made last year, I have no doubt that this tragic account of the girls' lives in Yemen is nothing less than conclusive proof of the accuracy of the details provided by Miss Ali."

He ends by demanding that the Foreign Office take "urgent steps" to bring the Muhsen girls home.

On the morning of 12 December, I phoned the Foreign Office to find out what sort of climate we could expect in Yemen. "It will be very cold," I was told. "Take lots of jumpers, gloves, etc." As I was packing, Miriam phoned again. "If you can't find Mohammed, try the postal agent, Nasser Saleh at the Post Office," she suggested. She had not slept, she said, trying to think of anyone else who might help.

I had my own list of other possible helpers. A colleague knew a couple who worked for a British company in Sana'a and gave me their telephone number. He also knew the Indian Ambassador, and telephoned him. He simply said that two of his friends were coming to Sana'a, and could the Ambassador arrange for someone to collect them? "No problem," said the Ambassador.

A Doctor Hisham El-Essay from the Islamic Society had telephoned the day before. He had read the articles in the last two weeks' papers and was disturbed to hear that we were planning to go to visit the girls. He thought that it would cause trouble. He said it would be much better if he could arrange meetings between leaders of Islam and the parents of the girls and their husbands, to sort it out as a "family matter". I said that Defence of Children had already tried this, to no avail, and that we were not going to cause trouble, just to find the girls and hear their story ourselves.

Another colleague had been in touch with a network of Embassy contacts and had given us the name of a British diplomat in Sana'a whom we could arrange to meet once we arrived. We were wary, after hearing from Miriam of the unhelpfulness of Mr Colin Page, of approaching the Embassy direct.

I also had tried the Red Cross and learnt that there was a Save the Children Fund representative in Taiz. I was given his name and telephone number, but was begged: "Please do not do anything that is going to endanger him."

Ben and I met in the office at noon. There, a colleague told us that he had heard through a contact that when Sir Geoffrey Howe had met up with Hattersley the previous day, Sir Geoffrey had said: "The last thing we want is some pesky newspaper going in there and stirring things up."

We were just about to do that very thing. Our real tickets had arrived, and after some comments about trying to sell each other off for camels, we left the office.

On our way in the taxi to the Embassy of the Yemen Arab Republic in South Street, Mayfair, we were still not certain that our visas would be granted. We dreaded having to go back to the office in a couple of hours to declare the mission unaccomplished.

We also feared that we might bump into the *Sunday Mirror* either at the Embassy or airport, or, worst of all, that they were already over there, and we would meet them on their way out with the story when we were just arriving.

Again, the Consular Department was deserted. The man was still drinking tea when we arrived, but our visas were neatly stamped in our passport. We paid the £20 visa fee and skipped out. We had four hours before our flight, which was just as well because Ben had forgotten to bring enough of the right sort of film and I had forgotten to bring any notebooks.

Chapter Seven

The flight to Sana'a left about an hour late. In the back of the Yemenia jet was an old man on a stretcher, skeletal-like. The air-stewardess told us he was dying and wanted to kiss the ground of his homeland before he did.

It was a long night; we had left just after seven in the evening from Gatwick and were due to arrive in Yemen at seven on Saturday morning. I slept for a couple of hours and missed the lights of Mecca.

Flying into Yemen early in the morning, with the sun blazing down on the arid landscape, was spectacular. We passed over mountains and desert, tracked by roads resembling mystical, prehistoric markings. The country, in its dryness, looked ancient, older than anything on earth. The houses, with ornate turrets, were like those sandcastles made from a square bucket and spade. As we touched down, the runway to one side was full of wrecked aircraft, painted in camouflage green. From the air they would appear as a squadron of fighter planes.

Stepping out of the aircraft we were hit by the heat and the bright dazzling light of the sun. It was meant to be cold, I thought, cursing the Foreign Office.

Inside the reception area of the airport, the Yemeni nationals passed quickly through immigration and customs. Westerners were told to go and change 150 dollars at the bank, just beside the door. The "bank" was a kiosk, in which two men stood. A piece of paper stuck on the window proclaimed: "The Bank of the Yemen Arab Republic". Once we had changed our money, we stood in the queue to have our visas checked. We were still wondering whether a hand would suddenly grab us and whisk us off out of the country. Miriam had said just before we left that she did not trust either Muthana or Gohad — if either got to hear about our trip, they would warn the authorities.

As we waited, there was a shout: "Mr Ben and Mrs Donald." This is it, we thought. But the official shouting our names, beyond the immigration points where armed guards stood, was smiling. Tentatively, we waved at him. He pushed through the bad-tempered queue. "You come from London?" he asked. We nodded. Better to get it over with. "Indian Ambassador's man here for you," he said, beaming. We beamed back.

Through the even more bad-tempered queue he pushed us until we were at the front. The guard took our passports and leafed through for the visas. Our official seemed angry that we were having to wait; he shouted at the guard, waving his hands. The guard, disgruntled, had one last stab at officialdom. "Tourists? How long in Yemen?"

"Oh, a week, maybe longer," said Ben. Our visas were actually valid for a month. The guard stamped in our entry visas, and our friendly official took us to customs.

A quick burst of shouting and arm waving, and our bags were chalked. Then an Indian man, who had been sitting in an office, came out and told us he was from the Indian Embassy. He hurried us through the throng of the waiting hall and we were outside. A black limousine stood waiting, its driver opening doors for us and putting our bags in the boot. The Indian diplomat clearly had no idea who we were. He said he was there to give us any assistance, but first, perhaps we would care to come back to the Embassy? We agreed. The first thing we wanted to do, apart from sleep, was contact the member of the British Embassy staff who we had been told may be helpful. We telephoned from the diplomat's office inside his Embassy. I asked if we could arrange to meet him, and he asked if we were journalists. We had decided to stay at the Taj Sheba Hotel, and suggested 7.30 the next morning. The Indian diplomat was now very curious, but politeness, or maybe diplomacy, stopped him asking too many questions. For his sake, anyway, we did not want him to know who we were.

He arranged for us to be taken to the hotel, a palatial building, where we booked in and slept until the afternoon. After eating, and when we were more or less awake, we decided that we had better try to look as much like tourists as possible. In a booklet we had managed to buy in London on travelling inside Yemen I had read that tourists had to get documentation in order to go outside Sana'a. We asked the woman behind the reception desk, who spoke excellent English, referring to everyone as "love", where we should go to get our travel documents. "The tourist office beside the old museum, love," she said. "But it is shut and will not open until the morning."

She told us that we would have to take our passports and an itinerary of where we wished to visit. We asked her what there was to see in Sana'a. "The old city, love," she said, rather peeved at such an ignorant question. We explained that we had come to visit the whole of Yemen, and would probably visit the old part of the city on our return. She was clearly displeased and with a withering look turned to another guest.

We went outside for a walk, and were immediately pounced upon by a pack of ravening taxi-drivers. An old man won, and shoved us into the back of his BMW. All the taxis were BMWs. He had decided to give us a tour of the city, and very expensive it proved too. All conversation was directed towards Ben. When I spoke he was given amazed looks as if he was expected to keep me silent. We were, everyone assumed, man and wife, in spite of having different surnames. It would be unthinkable that we should travel together unless we were married.

Sana'a, in late afternoon, was beginning to come to life. Street vendors displayed their wares on the pavements, veiled women walked in groups. Once or twice we saw women, entirely covered save for their eyes, just sitting in the road. "Not good women," was the explanation when we asked. Near the market, we asked the driver to stop, for we wanted to explore on our own. He was very put out, but finally agreed to let us go. We had told him we were planning to go down to Taiz the next morning and then to travel round sightseeing in the southern part of the country. He insisted on driving us down there. We were his friends now, he said.

Walking through the market, we saw that the Yemen was well stocked in things material. Hi-fi systems, radios and cameras jostled with stalls filled with fruit and vegetables, rolls of cloth, coffee, spices and toy stalls displaying prominently inflatable orange camels. We were waved to and beckoned over, offered tea before the messy business of buying. Groups of women averted their heads as we passed, or kept their eyes firmly fixed on the ground. The age of embarrassment seemed to be around eight-years-old. Below that girls stared after us, open-mouthed.

Occasionally I was spat at by an old, qat-chewing man, and when after buying pepsi-cola we had sat down on some steps to drink it, the spitting — at me — became fairly accurate. I don't know what they had against a woman sitting on a step, but it was clearly beyond the pale.

Soldiers and civilians armed with machine-guns wandered through the crowds. No one gave them a second glance; in Yemen until the last ten years the machine-gun was considered an essential part of everyday wear for men, a British expatriate told us. Still, it was unnerving to be poked in the arm by a passing Kalashnikov.

We returned to the hotel in the early evening and I decided to telephone the British couple whose names I had been given as friends of a journalist. I cannot name them, because the repercussions of what we did in Yemen are still going on, particularly towards British people, whose chief crime was that they spoke to us. The couple were keen to help when we told them that we had come to look for two British girls living in Mokbana. They said that they had heard of many British girls being sold as brides, but not these two in particular. We asked them if they knew anyone in the area of Taiz who might help. They gave us the name of a man and his telephone number. He worked all over the mountain area, they said, and even if he did not know the girls, he might know someone who had heard of them. They warned us of a few things: that the British community may be scared to help us because of National Security. We had probably been watched since the moment we landed, and no doubt followed. Don't trust taxi-drivers, we were told, they report to National Security; they are in their pay. The man told us that a British friend of theirs had been picked up by National Security because he chose to live in a rundown area of Sana'a and rode a bicycle to work. "They think that all Europeans are rich, and they thought this man must be up to no good because of his lifestyle. They took him in for interrogation and obviously did not believe a word he said. They even accused him of spying. And if you can imagine it, they tried to follow him for a bit when he was riding his bicycle. Basically, they haven't got much to occupy them, and a European doing anything out of the ordinary, like not simply being part of a tourist group, is fair game." He also warned us, a little belatedly, that it was not safe to speak on hotel telephones. He promised that he would telephone his friend in Taiz, and tell him that we would probably be contacting him.

He had given us a lot to think about, and a lot more to be jumpy about. We considered whether he was simply paranoid, but we were soon to learn this was not the case.

On Sunday, at 7.30 a.m., the British diplomat walked into the restaurant where we were having breakfast. We explained, for he was very curious how we had got hold of his name, that a colleague at *The Observer* had known a friend of his in Beirut. He asked if we had come about the Consular case. "Which one?" I asked, and he said that there was only one, so far as he knew. I told him about the Muhsen sisters, and he said: "That's the one." He then explained that he was nothing to do with the Consular side of the Embassy, and that we should really be talking to the Consul. We said that according to the mother, the Consul had been extremely unhelpful and that explained our reluctance to go to the Embassy direct.

He wanted to know what our plans were, so we told him that we hoped to find the girls and hear their story ourselves. He asked how we planned to set about finding them, and we said we knew the names of the villages, and hoped to find someone in Taiz who could help us get to them. We told him the names, but he said he had never heard of them, but that didn't mean they didn't exist, just that they were two of the hundreds of tiny villages scattered throughout Mokbana.

We got the impression that he did not think we had a hope — he asked if the expedition failed, was I planning to write about anything else during our stay — like the oil-wells?

He said that the politics of the country were far more interesting. There was feuding in the south near the border with communist-controlled South Yemen. The fighting, as often as not, was not between North and South, but between tribes. Occasionally North Yemen sent in its conscript army, and got beaten up by both sides. The President of North Yemen, he told us, was a master at "sitting on the fence". Yemen was a poor country and needed aid, and the current ruler took aid from whoever offered it. Consequently, there were Aid Projects, doctors, teachers, equipment and weaponry all flooding into his country from Russia, America, Libya, Egypt and Iran. No offer of help, whatever its source, was rejected. The President, a former soldier, who had overthrown his predecessor in the early 1980s, wore a civilian suit, but most Yemenis in private admitted their country was now a military state.

He repeated that he was not the person we should be talking to, and it was obvious that Consular matters were not his field. He was also concerned that we could get into trouble. He told us the story of an English woman, a student, who had recently been in Yemen and become another Consular case. "She was doing a thesis on village life in Yemen, and got the chance to interview a sheyekh (sheik) of a village. Rather foolishly she went off on her own with a driver. When she got to the village and met the sheyekh, he made some sort of rape attempt. It is unclear what happened but according to her the driver joined in as well. The police got involved, but it ended up with her being arrested — as a spy. The sheyekh accused her of it, and his word was taken against hers. Things could have got very nasty indeed for her, but in the end she was fined something like 12,000 rials and asked to leave the country, which she did very promptly."

We were going into a very similar situation, into remote mountain villages, far from a telephone call to the British Embassy. But at least we were a couple, and assumed to be man and wife. "Have you got a ring?" the diplomat asked. I showed my engagement ring to him. We told him we hoped to set off for Taiz later in the morning, and he asked us to keep him informed if we had any news.

We felt despondent after he had gone. Wary of approaching the uncaring Mr Page, even thinking that the Embassy might decide it was better not to have two journalists around, particularly bearing in mind Sir Geoffrey Howe's dislike of "pesky newspapers", we feared that the Embassy might even report us to the authorities.

We decided that we were very much on our own, and that we

would have to rely on the man in Taiz and the representative of
the Save the Children Fund for the time being. We set out for a
brisk walk to the Old Museum to sort out our travel permits, but
we reckoned without our taxi-driver. Once again we were
manhandled into his car and driven in a roundabout fashion to
the Old Museum.

It was open. Armed guards sat in a hut outside, but when we
said we were tourists they nodded us through. The building was
ancient, built of stone and very cool inside; the tourist office was
tucked away within the building. Two men sat in the office,
having what seemed to us a dreadful argument, but was in fact
probably a mild discussion on the weather. We had to fill up
forms saying where we wanted to go. A map we had bought in
London showed that Mokbana lay between Taiz and Al Mokha
on the coast.

To put any official off we had also chosen some other places
around Taiz: Al Tourbah, very close to the border with
communist South Yemen and purportedly extremely beautiful,
with a view over the mountains into the other half of Yemen;
Hajjah, a town north of Sana'a; and fairly close-by, Tulla and
Shibam, two places we had been told were well worth seeing. In
the south we said we wanted to visit Zabad, simply because it was
in block capitals on the map, and Ibb, north-east of Taiz.

The itinerary was fairly comprehensive, and we were asked
how long we wished to stay. "Until our money runs out," I said,
indicating our visas showing one month's duration. Our intended
route would have to be translated into Arabic, written on to the
official form and stamped. We were told to go and look around
the museum shop.

It was full of the most exquisite, ancient-looking silver
jewellery. Ben and I decided that we would pay a visit at the end
of our journey to buy Christmas presents. Unfortunately as
things turned out we were not to be in a position to do so.

We went back to collect our papers, now duly stamped. There
had been no problem, everything we had asked for, even
Mokbana was marked down. Our next task was to get
photocopies of the permit — around 50, our man on the
telephone in Sana'a had told us. Each time we passed a road-
block, and there would be probably a dozen or so on the road

Eileen MacDonald

down to Taiz, we would need to hand one over to the soldiers, who would in turn give them to Security. I remembered that Miriam had vaguely talked of road-blocks and that she had just shown her passport — but then she had been a mother visiting her daughters, not a tourist. It was only later that we were told that most of the soldiers on road-block duty were illiterate and therefore ignorant of what the permits said.

When we emerged from the Old Museum our taxi-driver broke his golden rule of travelling everywhere by car, and said he would take us ON FOOT to the photocopying shop. It was only 20 yards away, it turned out, so it would have been difficult even for him to give us a tour driving us there.

We were charged a phenomenal amount for the photocopies — around £30 — but we did not want to create a scene involving the police. On our way back to the Taj Sheba Hotel to check out, however, we had a conspiratorial conversation in the back seat. This man was not going to take us to Taiz — we would never get there, we thought, for he would insist on taking us for tours.

It was about 10 a.m., and if we were going to catch the representative of the Save the Children Fund at his clinic before two in the afternoon, we had to be in Taiz in under four hours. We told the old man that we needed a very fast driver to take us to Taiz and he seemed affronted. He said it could only be done in four-and-a-half to five hours, but if (extremely huffily) we wanted to be "fast, fast", four hours might be possible. Just to show us what he was made of, he put his foot down and we screeched back to our hotel at 60 mph, narrowly missing the odd pedestrian.

We checked out swiftly and insisted on another driver. Great arguments, hysteria arose. Then the old man, who appeared to be the king of the taxi-rank, sulkily pushed forward a younger man who worked for him. Sultan. Sultan would take us to Taiz for 300 dollars. We tried to barter, but it produced the entire hotel staff, shouting at us that this was a fair price. It was only later in the week we were told there was a regular flight to Taiz, taking around 25 minutes and costing £16. As far as we knew, taxi was the only way and we agreed to the fare.

Chapter Eight

Sultan, a smiling, curly-headed young man, took us at our word and drove "fast, fast" for about the first hour, only halting at the road-blocks. Our permits passed muster for the qat-chewing guards. Ben decided that he wanted a picture of one of the guards, in full gun-toting kit. But this did not go down at all well. He tried all sorts of different techniques: the jolly British tourist innocently snapping away — that nearly resulted in arrest; getting me out of the car to stand by a guard — the guard ran a mile; then finally asking Sultan if he could stop the car some little way from the next road-block so that he could take a picture without the guards noticing. Sultan became alarmed: "No, no, not good," he said. Then not wishing to offend his wealthy passengers, he pointed to some camels that were eating a tree: "Camels," he said brightly. "Pictures."

To appease him Ben dutifully got out to take photographs of the beasts. That created a minor uproar, as everyone in the village descended on him, shouting, "Kodak, Kodak", roughly interpreted as "take a picture of me". Two of those descending from the village happened to be men with machine-guns slung over their shoulders. But they had not come shouting Kodak, they were there to keep an eye on things. When Ben tried to take their photograph, they became angry, pushing him away, trying to get the camera. In the car, Sultan asked me: "Why does he want to take photographs of the gunmen?" I said that he was an artist, a photography student, and he wanted pictures of every aspect of life in Yemen. "But the mountains, the camels, yes, the guns not good," said Sultan.

He got out of the car to rescue Ben from the mob, but Ben had gone in search of women to photograph. He needed as much colour of the place as possible in case we were unsuccessful in our attempt to find the girls, and I had to write a general piece on the sort of society the girls were living in. But trying to take photographs of women was an even more impossible task than gun pictures. The women shied away; the men became angry.

Back in the car Ben told me: "I had got into the market, and there was a woman with her face unveiled. I just raised the camera, then down came the veil and I nearly got eaten by a man beside me."

Sultan explained to him: "No woman must allow her picture. Very bad." He was clearly puzzled as to why his passenger was trying to take illegal photographs — and no doubt a bit worried too, for if his passengers got arrested, he would be in trouble for collaborating with them. "Mr Ben, you must be careful," he said. "Men with guns, no, women, no, anything else, good pictures."

Beside me, Ben growled. "Those are the only pictures I want, chum," he said. For the next hour or so, with me acting the long-suffering female, he told Sultan how he wanted to get those pictures because no one else had, and he wanted to be a famous photography student.

With my eyes rolling heavenward frequently, I chimed in, saying to Sultan: "Always, he tries to take such photographs. He leaves me standing in a street, and disappears."

Sultan cottoned on. "Mr Ben mad picture-man," he said. This settled, he ceased to be so worried when Ben asked for the car to stop and went walkabout in villages.

The drive from Sana'a to Taiz on the wide German and Chinese-built roads, was unforgettable. Sultan was a good driver, only overtaking when he could see a clear stretch. This did not seem to be the case with many of his countrymen. They appeared to drive at full speed, overtaking on mountain roads, with a predilection for doing so on corners when the road vanished round the mountain. Wrecks of cars were everywhere, as were small aircraft, even once a helicopter. "He went into the mountain," said Sultan.

His English was quite good; we did not know how much he could understand, so we quizzed him about it, congratulating him at first. He visibly swelled with pride. "I go to school at nights," he said. "I come to England, maybe next year."

"You must come to stay with us," we said, determined not to give him our addresses. He beamed more. Did we, he asked, speak Arabic? I had worked for an Arabic newspaper as my first job in journalism, but had learned very little of the language, my chief duties being to make coffee and open doors. Please, thank-you, hello, how are you, were just about the extent of my Arabic. Sultan was delighted. "Good wife," he said to Ben.

"You must be joking," said Ben, smiling and nodding.

But there was one more phrase I knew: "Don't shoot me. I'm only a journalist." I had learnt it when I was in Libya in 1985 on two of Terry Waite's missions to free four British hostages taken after the Libyan Embassy siege. The men assigned to guarding the press corps then had taught it to us, they said as a joke. We had not been so sure, and had all taught ourselves to be fluent with the phrase. I remember being particularly proud of learning the words for female journalist: "Sahafia", or at least that was what it sounded like. Sitting in the back of the car, concentrating on the few words of Arabic I knew, I started saying the phrase and just caught myself in time. "I forget," I said to Sultan, who thankfully had not heard.

For a time we just sat taking in the scenery. It really was beautiful. We were passing through a mountain range over 3,300 metres high. Way down below us we could see the "wadis", river valleys, with the sliver of water making the scenery it ran through green. The couple we had called in Sana'a told us that they often took off in a jeep to explore the wadis, going far into the interior of the country. It would have been wonderful. The sides of some of the mountains were dotted with tiny stone houses. Occasionally we saw boys tending a few scrawny goats, or a girl looking after sheep. The animals were amazing, nimbly climbing the mountains, leaving their young masters on a piece of rock.

Passing through one remote village I saw a young girl, in colourful dress, standing beside what looked to be a hard plastic water tank. She would be about seven years of age. Beside her towered her father, ladling out water from the tank into her pot, before sending her off over the edge of the mountain, presumably to her home. She was as sure-footed as the goats, her pot steady on her small head.

In the back of the car Ben and I had decided that it was just possible that Sultan understood quite a lot of what we said. Bearing in mind the words of the previous day, that he could just possibly be in the pay of National Security, or duty-bound to report strange tourists, we launched into a loud conversation about the beauty of Yemen, and how we wanted to visit all over. I said that I wanted to buy material and old silver as presents, and how we really must get around to buying postcards for home. We discussed our imaginary home, and how we had so many spare rooms for friends we met on our travels around the world. If Sultan did understand our talk, he gave no sign, happy to join in when we asked him a direct question.

We could see from the time that it was unlikely we were going to make Taiz before the Save the Children Fund clinic closed. We asked Sultan to put his foot down, but he said "Dangerous" and we could see his point. He told us that he lived in Taiz, and had only moved to Sana'a to get work. "No work in Taiz," he said, but added that he liked to go home to see his family as often as he could.

Perhaps it had been a mistake to mention time, because it was coming up to 12.30 p.m., and Sultan stopped the car at a remote village that just seemed to cling on to the mountainside by its teeth. "Lunch, not long," he said.

"Sultan," I said. "We have to get to Taiz before two o'clock."

"No problem," he said then disappeared into a shop-cum-home. He was immediately surrounded by men, hugging and kissing him. We realised that these must be some of his relatives, but looking at our map, saw that we were only just halfway. We had to resign ourselves to waiting until the next day to telephone our clinic contact.

We both got out of the car, Ben to try taking photographs of a few of the women — again no luck, but Sultan this time showed little concern except to laugh at Ben and say something along the lines of "He's just nuts" to the village men. I still found it uncomfortable being stared at by the men. I was hardly wearing a revealing bikini, after all. Because of the Foreign Office instruction to bring warm clothes, I had two pairs of thick cord trousers, and a pair of cotton trousers. I was wearing these, with boots of all things, in temperatures approaching 90 degrees Fahrenheit. I also wore a long-sleeved blouse, buttoned to the neck, and had sunglasses on. Pretty safe, I would have thought. I was only to learn from the British Ambassador's wife at the end of the week that my problem was I tucked the blouse into my trousers. I should have been wearing it outside. I got very fed up being touched, stared at and shouted at by men. The women, I noticed, would turn their heads away with a sort of scandalised sneer.

I got back into the car to wait. Little children, growing curious, came to stare in through the window, asking for something I could not understand. I thought it was money, but later learned that it was pencils or pens so that they could write at school. Apparently pens, even biros, were not simply very expensive, but hard to get, and it was a great status symbol to own one, rather than use chalk on slates in the classroom.

Ben meanwhile was at the heart of a Kodak-shouting throng. The men, although willing to kill to guard against their women being captured on camera, were jostling to get to the front of the queue. What was funny was that after Ben had obliged, they demanded money for the privilege. He finally joined me in the car because he was in danger of using up too much film. We had, I thought, masses of rolls. He had given me about 20 rolls to carry in my bag in case, for any reason, his were confiscated.

Sultan, after about an hour, returned. We had by then resigned ourselves to passing a night in the village. He brought us pepsis and lamb in pitta bread. We were pretty hungry, but when I looked inside the bread I saw green meat, or what looked like it. It was in fact the animal's fat, and the sheep had been killed in our honour. It must have been an elderly sheep, I thought, as we chewed it.

Sultan seemed in bouncy mood. He was carrying with him a bundle of what resembled privet hedge branches. This was our first sighting of qat before it got chewed. Sultan was chewing, and as he started to drive off, offered us some. Ben, to be manly and polite, took some leaves, but put them in the pocket of his jeans. Something that our British diplomat had told us the previous morning was that the qat, grown in the mountain villages, was sprayed with DDT. "Wash it first," he had said with English *savoir-faire*. He had also told us that everyone in Yemen chewed qat, the men openly, the women in the private of their homes.

He said that it was actually considered an insult not to chew if offered the leaves. He had been concerned at what the attitude of the Foreign Office might be if they knew their diplomats had to chew the stuff — which had a similar effect to the drug known in Britain as "Speed". "I was shocked at first when I went to a Foreign Affairs' Ministry official's home, and found him chewing," he said. "But it is the done thing, like having a drink."

Sultan was highly amused at Ben's reluctance to chew. I was safe enough, for as a woman it was seemly not to chew in public. Ben explained that he felt a bit car-sick, but Sultan clearly took this as a weak excuse. "When I chew," he said with bulging cheek, "I never need to sleep, I don't need to eat. Very good." This probably explained why all the men, for it was impossible to tell what a woman looked like clad in her tent-like dress, had such nimble figures. They did not look particularly healthy, but they were all skinny.

Finally we began to descend from the mountains. Sultan told us that Taiz was not far, but we had come to realise he told us what he thought we wanted to hear. Time, appointments in Yemen were unimportant. "Al bukra" — tomorrow — accompanied by the shrug of the shoulders, would do.

We were now passing fields, deeply furrowed, though still at a height of 3,000 metres. We asked how it was done, for we had seen no tractors and the Yemeni farmers did not appear to have ploughs. "Tyres," said Sultan.

"You mean they roll the tyres up and down?" asked Ben. Sultan nodded.

His driving had become less good, though he seemed full of beans. One or two sharp mountain bends had been taken at break-neck speed — presumably the effect of qat. He kept adding more leaves to his mouth, but not spitting out those he already had in there. Occasionally he would spit out of the windows. Throughout Yemen we saw dried green liquid on the ground, the result of the population's chief pastime.

Eventually our journey, which had taken nearly six hours, came to an end. We had reached Taiz. Smaller than Sana'a, it had a friendlier, more bustling atmosphere. We drove slowly through the market area, where school must just have finished. We saw dozens of small girls in grey uniform, with a sort of nun's

head-dress in white covering their hair and shoulders. I pointed
to them and asked Sultan if all girls went to school in Yemen.
"Only the rich ones," he said.

He had decided which hotel we were staying in — the Mareb.
I tried to get him to go to the Hotel Ganad, the one that Miriam
had told me was opposite the Post Office. Sultan was shocked.
"Not for tourists," he said. I insisted that he take us there,
because I wanted to see where the Post Office was, so that, if we
could get help from no other quarter, we could try Miriam's
suggestion of the postal agent or Zana's brother-in-law.

I had decided on our journey that it would be a risk to try either
man. Miriam might have found help with them, but then she was
a relative of the girls. I feared that they would find a simple way
out by informing National Security if a couple of tourists turned
up and asked to be taken to the girls. Even if they were themselves
frightened of involving the authorities they could easily block our
attempts to get to the villages by warning of our arrival so that we
ran into an ambush. Even worse, if they thought we had come to
rescue the girls, they could move them far away and we would
never find them.

But if all our contacts failed and we had to resort to the men,
at least I wanted to know where to find them, and the Hotel
Ganad was on the doorstep. Very reluctantly, and tutting through
his qat, Sultan took us to the hotel. I went inside, but discovered
its main disadvantage, apart from being filthy, was it had no
telephones. Sultan looked smug when I emerged, shaking my
head.

With an "I told you so" expression, he drove us up a very steep
hill to the Mareb Hotel. From the outside it looked most
impressive, dominating the city. Inside it was shabby, the staff
were sullen and the building was devoid of air-conditioning. But
at least it had telephones. There was also a bar, we discovered,
that sold alcohol of a sort — bootleg whisky — but only to
tourists. Good Muslims, we were told, were forbidden to drink,
so that the Mareb Hotel Bar was notorious in town and often full
of drinking tourists.

We wanted to relax for a while, walk round town, and make plans.
Sultan seemed anxious not to leave our sides, but we insisted that
we would be quite capable of going for a walk on our own.

We unpacked then met in my room for a talk on what to do next. We thought that Sultan was probably safe, and seemed to like us. Why not get him to take us to the villages direct in the morning? It was a risk, but if he was the genuine taxi-driver he appeared, possibly less of a risk than getting other people involved. I had the names of the villages in Mokbana written down — Hockail and Shubee. We decided that after our walk we would ask Sultan to take us in the morning.

Taiz had a wonderful market, reached at one end by passing through an ancient archway. Immediately you were in the spice section of the market and a little further on in the date section. By this time it was early evening, and we were hungry, but wary of eating straight from the market. Peanuts were being cooked in furnaces, and offered to us. These seemed safe enough, in fact they were delicious.

Ben decided that I should try with a camera to snatch some pictures of women. Maybe they would not be so frightened of a woman taking their photographs. I did manage to get some shots, but unfortunately I did not know how to use the camera, so they came out as a blur. The men on the other hand seemed on the verge of apoplexy when I pointed the camera at them.

When we got back to the hotel, Sultan was waiting for us, clearly relieved to see that his troublesome charges were still in one piece. We said that tomorrow we wanted to visit some friends of ours. Would he take us?

"Yes, of course," he said, probably thinking, "Yum, yum, lots more money."

"They are two small villages in Mokbana," I said.

Sultan's face fell. "No, not Mokbana," he said firmly. "Bad place."

"Sultan, we are going to Mokbana, we have promised our friends' family and we have gifts and letters from them."

Sultan shook his head, but we kept insisting. Finally, with a deep sigh, he nodded. But he said: "Not this car. We must get another."

He said he thought he knew someone who had a car which would go into Mokbana and he would take us to the man. He drove us down into town, through a bewildering array of tiny, unmade roads, into the poor quarter of the city. He stopped at a house, and got out. After ten minutes or so, he was back, with two other men. They had a jeep, he said. We would all go together. He wanted to know the names of the villages, so I told him. All the men shook their heads. They had never heard of Shubee, or Hockail.

Our hearts sunk. Had Miriam got it wrong? Had she deliberately given us the wrong names because the *Sunday Mirror* had paid her? Was the whole thing a hoax?

But one of the men suddenly exclaimed: "Ashube! Ashube!" We were back in business. Not Shubee, as Miriam had said, but Ashube, and Okile. Everyone was suddenly terribly pleased — Sultan and his friends were delighted to have solved our problem. But no one was more pleased than Ben and I. The possibility of the places not existing was a thought just too horrible to contemplate. One of Sultan's friends wrote down in my notebook the names of the villages.

The jeep would be ready at our hotel at eight o'clock the following morning. Sultan would come with us — he insisted upon it — plus the two other men. The cost was going to be horrendous, but if all went well, it was going to be worth it.

Chapter Nine

We returned to the hotel, relieved, but still feeling nervous. The warning that taxi-drivers could be spies was still hanging over our heads. We were aware that we were trusting Sultan with an awful lot.

It was still only early evening, and I remembered that our Sana'a contact had telephoned his friend in Taiz and that this man was probably waiting to hear from us. To safeguard him and his family, I shall call him David, and his wife, Carol. Back in my hotel room, I telephoned David and we arranged to go to their house at about 7.30 p.m. that evening.

David and Carol had lived in Taiz for some ten years, and his job meant that he worked daily with Yemeni people. He spoke Arabic well, and had a wealth of information about local customs.

When we arrived at his beautiful home, half way up a mountain just outside Taiz, an astonishing variety of drinks was offered to us, in this a dry Muslim country. David explained that the alcohol was mainly smuggled in through Al Mokha on the coast, via Cyprus.

His wife joined us, and we quickly got down to business. We told David and Carol what we were planning to do the next day, and they said we were utterly mad. David in fact was very angry at what he saw as our stupidity in attempting to simply roll up on the girls' doorsteps.

"I can only assume it is your ignorance of the whole Yemeni culture that has made you think of such an idea," he said. "You will either never get there, or you will be shot, or imprisoned. You should both just go home now."

It was quite a blow to be told this when in fact we thought we had been rather clever. David turned to Ben: "You certainly might as well just go home now," he said. "You won't get within yards of the girls with a camera. The men will lynch you. Teach her (*nodding at me*) to use your camera. She has got a chance of getting in, but not with a man, and a Western man at that."

He then went on to tell us what we would be running into, if in the morning we persisted with our crazy plan. "As soon as you get into Mokbana, the villagers will put up their own road-blocks," he said. "These villagers are very independent people. They are armed. If they think you are dangerous they will kill you."

He told us the story about people going into the region to conduct a census and never coming back. I said that perhaps we would get through the village road-blocks with our tourist permits. This was scorned. "They will take no notice of those. The soldiers on the official road-blocks will read them, if they can, but the Mokbana people are different. Every village has a sheyekh, he is his own law-maker. You must get his permission first before you talk to anyone in his village, particularly the women. They would think he (*nodding to Ben*) had come to rape them.

"Even if you got to the villages, the women in them would hide the girls away. You would never see them. You journalists make me sick coming here and thinking you can just bulldoze your way in. Think of all the trouble you would cause the British community here if you did do a story. Just forget the whole thing."

We were sitting there, at this point, like a pair of burst balloons. This man was supposed to be helping us — we felt we were wasting our time, and were getting more depressed as the minutes passed. His wife interrupted. She said: "We have tried to help you today. We have been in touch with another family in Taiz, who do know the Mokbana area very well. One of their family does a lot of work with the villagers there, and we have asked her if it would be possible for her to speak to the sheyekh, and then talk to the girls to find out how they are. It may just be possible that if she has not already gone this afternoon to speak to them, that you may go with her tomorrow."

"Not him though," interjected her husband. "Only her, and then she must be careful to do nothing that could arouse suspicion."

David obviously had zero confidence in us. I got out some photocopies of newspaper cuttings about the girls' story. Two were from the *The Observer*; a couple from the tabloid press. This had the effect of making David even wilder. His voice rising to a shout, he said: "Bloody marvellous, this." He was clutching a cutting with a headline about sex slaves. "Sheer, bloody ignorance — just to sell bloody newspapers," he screamed. He grabbed the story from the *The Observer*. "Look at this," he waved it at Carol. "'Sana'a is 50 miles from Taiz.' Get your bloody geography right, girl."

I said, as evenly as I could, that there were no detailed maps of Yemen available when I wrote that, and besides the girls' mother had told me this was the distance, and she had travelled to Yemen.

"Why do you believe her story then?" he demanded. "We get a lot of these women. They agree to sell off their kids here, and then start screaming about it. You have no idea about this country. You're wet behind the ears, and all you care about is your pathetic story, which doesn't sound to me as if it's true. There are dozens of girls, no, hundreds, living in Mokbana from the Birmingham area. That's why they call it 'Little Birmingham'. One problem you won't have in Mokbana is no one understanding you. Every village has at least a couple of people who have either been to Britain, or been brought here."

I thought he was calming down slightly, so I asked if there were many girls brought out as brides. "Hundreds," was the curt reply. "Some are happy; lots aren't." Then he turned again. "Why believe this story and risk your lives? You are being set up, don't you see? Why don't you get to know the country first? Visit some hospitals, schools, old villages — even meet some British people like us who are happy here."

His wife interrupted to say that she had no Yemeni friends, and understood very little Arabic; in fact she was quite lonely.

Her husband silenced her. "You have the kid to look after," he said. "There are old age pensioners in Taiz who draw their pension every Thursday. They are happy here. Did you know that? No, of course you didn't. You don't want to know. You just want to write your sex story and get out of here leaving us to clear up the shit.

"There are British women in Taiz who are very happily married to Yemeni men, but you don't want to know about that either, do you?"

It was at about this point that I had the urge to tip the remainder of my gin and tonic over his head. But I refrained. I said that we did not have much time in which to investigate the truth of the story and therefore we obviously had to take risks to get to the girls quickly. I said that I would very much like to meet the pensioners and the happily married British women, and if, as he was forecasting, our journey in the morning proved to be fruitless, then that might well be the story I wrote for *The Observer*.

I had the feeling that he was not listening to a word that either Ben or I said. I thought that he had probably loathed journalists for years, and then, lo and behold, two turn up on his doorstep in the remote depths of Yemen, and he has captured them. I said that, having listened to the mother of the girls, read some of their letters and talked briefly to their father, I believed the story. I said that I had a tape-recording with me of one of the sisters telling their story, and if he would care to listen to it, he would at least know the facts as told by her.

"I don't want to hear your story," he sneered. "Play it to me afterwards, after you have done a good story about Yemen."

Later, when I told both the couple we had originally telephoned in Sana'a, and Neila, who knew David slightly, how he had acted, they were amazed. We came to the conclusion he had been hitting the contraband alcohol heavily before we arrived.

When he was not ranting about our ignorance and profession, he provided some interesting insights into life in Yemen. Everything could be got by bribes. Alcohol was permitted in the home, but you were liable to be very heavily fined, or even imprisoned if you were found transporting it. He told us about the Beheading Square in Taiz. "It's the taxi rank," he said. "Whenever they are going to chop someone's head off, they move the taxis away. We were in Taiz one day recently when soldiers rolled up to the taxi ranks in great lorries. 'Oh no,' I thought, 'I must get out of here.' Before I could, the taxis had been moved, and the soldiers started unlocking the lorries. But instead of bringing out a string of prisoners, they started throwing off crates of booze. Then they got out their daggers and beheaded the bottles. They have purges like that occasionally, and the smugglers go underground for a while. Then it starts up again."

He added, in this lucid spell, that he was aware that the hand was still cut off for certain crimes. There was another place in Taiz, he said, where the ground was stained with blood. He would take us there. So far I had not seen anyone minus a hand in Yemen. I told David this. He said: "But how many people have you seen with just one arm?" I agreed I had seen quite a few, but presumed they had been in a war or an accident. "No," he said. "The shame of having your hand chopped off and being marked forever as a thief is so great that they get a friend, or surgeon if they can bribe him, to remove the arm."

He told us that in the last five years great advances had been made in the living standards for the ordinary Yemeni. Today education was available to all, although mainly only boys were allowed to go to school — girls being too useful at home to work generally and to look after younger children. Boys, it appeared, were quickly trained in basic educational skills of literacy and numeracy, although many still left school at 12 years old. At "prep" school age, that is between 12 and 15, 12 per cent of those attending were girls. At secondary level, 15 to 18 years old, it dropped slightly to ten per cent. David and Carol told us that they had some Yemeni friends whose children were still attending school in their twenties. "Money runs out, or the kids are needed at home for a while, so the education is interrupted," said David. "It is very common in Yemen for students in secondary or even prep schools to be married men with families."

Keeping David off the story we were in the country to get seemed the best way to have a sensible conversation. I asked him next about qat. "Everyone does it," he said. "The amazing thing is that it is very expensive. One bundle of qat that would do for one chewing session costs around 500 rials. That is about £40. The pay of a quite professional person is 3,000 rials a month, so you can see qat is not a cheap addiction."

Ben and I tentatively reintroduced our trip. We felt that what David had told us, irrespective of his insults, about the dangers we would be facing in the morning, might be worth heeding.

"How would it be," I said, "if we managed to go with this lady tomorrow to the villages and speak to the sheyekh? We could tell him that we had messages and presents for the girls from home, and that we promised their mother we would see they were delivered personally."

This time, David did not explode. "I suppose it is one way. You could get to the village checkpoint, and say you wished to speak to the sheyekh. In fact he (*nodding to Ben*) would have to request the meeting, because the sheyekh would never agree to talk to a woman. As long as you did not attempt to get past the road-block and just march in unasked, it might be all right."

Ben and I decided to take a brief walk in the garden to talk things over. We both felt very angry at the insults which had been flung at us, unfairly, we considered. But the man, although rabid in his hatred for journalists, obviously knew the place much better than us. To ignore what he had told us about the armed villagers and road-blocks would be foolhardy. We decided that we would cancel the trip, speak to the family Carol had mentioned as soon as we could in the morning, and arrange, if possible, to go with the lady into the villages. We felt defeated. We knew we were now facing the prospect of not seeing the girls; that we might have to rely on this lady whom we did not know to interview the girls on our behalf. Carol had told us she was dual nationality, her mother being British and her father Yemeni. We did not know if she would be prepared to risk the work she did with the Mokbana people to help us. She might be inarticulate, bring back as the sole message from the girls' villages: "They are all right." And Ben of course had been told in no uncertain terms that he might as well send his cameras home on the next available flight. It was pretty depressing.

Carol seemed very relieved when we returned and said that we had agreed to put off our trip. She promised that she would telephone us the following evening at the hotel as soon as she had spoken to the family. "I don't think the daughter went off to Mokbana today," she said. "It is 11 o'clock, too late to phone them now. I will speak to them tomorrow and say that you wish to go too. They are good people, they will help."

David became much pleasanter once he knew we were taking his advice. He suggested that we spend the day visiting the "real

Yemen". Al Tourbah, which I knew we had on our tourist permits, was a couple of hours away, he said, and had spectacular mountains, dropping for thousands of feet into South Yemen. We decided we might as well try.

When we got back to the Mareb Hotel, we sat up talking long into the night. We were making contingency plans for a different story, as it now appeared the one we had come for was going to prove impossible to get. A general piece on the British expatriate community, I thought, with particular reference to old folks drawing their pension from Taiz Post Office. It did not grab us as a story. A colour piece then on Mokbana, based on the stories we had heard? It might have to be that in the end. But we both felt that to have got this close to the sisters, and then give up, was impossible. We finally resolved, at about 3 a.m., that if this family in Taiz would not help us we would go in on our own on Wednesday.

In the morning we had to do a great deal of paying-off. Sultan's two friends, and the jeep, and a bit extra, demanded Sultan, for the inconvenience. Just to really irritate him, we told him that after today we would not need him any more. One thing that Carol had told us was that we were being charged about triple the normal rate, although it was to be expected as we were supposedly tourists. We drove to Al Tourbah, with a sulky cloud hanging over Sultan's head. We were not feeling like Easter bunnies either.

When we got to Al Tourbah, it was, as David had said, worth seeing. The village was about 20 yards from the edge of a sheer drop. Hundreds of feet below us, eagles circled. The children in the village played on this mountain drop as if it was their playground, which I suppose it was. They seemed to run up and down the mountain. We had acquired a guide, a teacher at the village school, who told us that it was very rare that anyone fell off. The children, he said seemed to know by instinct, even as toddlers, of the mountain's dangers.

The teacher was extremely hospitable. He took us into his home, introduced us to his wife and two children. She prepared lunch for us, our first true Yemeni meal, sitting cross-legged on foam mattresses on the floor. He seemed to completely accept our story that we were simply tourists, and Ben's cameras fascinated him. We were shown all the family's albums. But all the while we were nagged by the thought of what was going to happen. We felt we were going to fail.

The teacher asked us if we would do him the honour of visiting his school. It was purpose-built, modern, he said, and catered for children for many miles around. It was still only just after noon, and we agreed. On the short walk he said that the village had been recently plagued by thieves, but they had been caught and punished. We asked how, had they been imprisoned?

"No," said the teacher. "They were blown up." This seemed extreme, but he explained. "They had air pumped into them from the rear." Ben and I paled. I said it seemed very barbaric; the teacher replied: "It is better than losing the hand."

His school was built round a courtyard: low cement buildings with the Yemeni flag flying from a pole in the centre. Our arrival caused a sensation. The students, mostly in their early teens, tumbled out of the buildings and we were surrounded. Everyone was trying out their English. The teacher, who turned out to be the headmaster, restored order after a while, and then invited us in to speak to the classes. It was funny, in retrospect. There we were, sneaking around the country as journalists, worried to death about the story, and we were suddenly called upon to give a speech to six different classes of Yemeni schoolchildren.

On each metal door the headmaster knocked. Ben and I shuffled our feet, wishing we were anywhere but here. In we were led. "This is the biology lesson," explained the headmaster. On the blackboard was the drawing of a heart. The classroom was dark and cramped. The students varied in age from about 14 to 30 years of age. Right at the back, at a separate table, sat two girls, their eyes visible only, everything else shrouded. All the students had leapt to their feet.

The headmaster continued: "This is Mr Ben and his wife, Mrs Ben. They have come from England to see you. Has anyone got any questions they would like to ask our guests?"

A youth stood up, about three feet away from us. "How many babies have you got?" he asked. Well, it was a biology lesson. The class looked most unimpressed when Ben said, "None."

Then another student stood up. He was a young man. "I have three children," he said haltingly. Then he added in much better English: "How is the Queen?"

She was fine, we said, although we had not seen her recently. Other questions flowed thick and fast then. Was it raining in England? Did we like Yemen? Had we been in any other country? One youth said he was planning to come to England soon, but had nowhere to stay. Another one to forget giving our address to.

I asked the headmaster if I could speak to the two girls, who sat quietly at the back, with their eyes lowered. "Yes, anything," he said, beaming. I asked them if they enjoyed school. They were overcome with embarrassment and could not answer. "Yes, they like school very much," said the headmaster.

Ben asked if he could take a photograph of the class. I knew what he was after — the girls. The headmaster was all smiles; the boys delighted. But the girls, when he started to focus, suddenly got up, came to the front of the class, talked to the headmaster and walked out. "I am sorry. They say their fathers would be angry," he explained to us. Ben had to take the photograph anyway, with the only subjects he was interested in almost weeping with shyness outside.

By our sixth class we were old hands and it would have been almost enjoyable if the whole situation was not so ludicrous. We thanked the headmaster profusely and said we had to go back to Taiz. We had telephone calls to make which would wait no longer.

Chapter Ten

When I got back to my hotel room, Carol phoned with the telephone number of the Taiz family she thought could help us. She told us to wait a couple of hours before contacting them. Ben and I decided that in case we were able to go with a woman into the villages in the morning and anything should go wrong, then the Embassy ought to know of our plans.

We telephoned our diplomat. He told us: "I have reported our meeting on Sunday to the Ambassador, and he wishes to emphasise to you that what you propose could be highly dangerous. If you go into the villages, and the men mistake your reasons for being there, it may not just be imprisonment you face, you could be physically at risk — shot."

He also warned that our visit could have disastrous consequences for the girls; that they could be moved. "Look," he said. "We have got one Consular case on our hands already; we don't want you two as our second."

I said that we were still determined to visit the girls, but promised that, if we were able to get into the villages the next day, we would telephone him as soon as we came out. If we failed to contact him the following evening, we gave him instructions that our office should be alerted that we had gone missing.

We were spooked by the warning we had been given. We telephoned the office next and told them about it. Our instructions were clear: "Go to the villages, but if anyone stops you on the way, don't argue, don't be brave, just turn back."

Back in Birmingham, that day, the *Post* newspaper had run a story, headlined "Yemeni sisters face little hope of help". It was a report of a meeting between Mr Roy Hattersley and the Yemeni Ambassador in London. The Ambassador said that he held out little hope of helping the sisters, but suggested they could get a divorce. Mr Hattersley was reported as saying that this did not seem a very likely possibility because the girls were completely isolated. It was a very gloomy report. It was just as well that Ben and I, still feeling that the chance of our finding the girls was very remote, had no way of seeing it.

The hour had come to phone the family in Taiz. Because of the repercussions the publication of the story has already had on this family — arrest and interrogation — I have to disguise not only their identity but also pass over some of the tremendous help they gave us. They know who they are, and we are very grateful to them; I am only sorry I cannot write fully of the extent of their bravery to help the sisters.

Mrs X had a soft, Cardiff accent. She and her husband, a Yemeni, had lived in the country for many years. They had several children, some of them nurses. One of her daughters knew Mokbana well. She worked in the area and had heard of the sisters, although she had never seen them. Mrs X would come to our hotel at 7.30 p.m. and we could talk then.

We were in the restaurant when she arrived. She was wearing red and picked us out easily as we were the only Europeans in the room. We finished our meal quickly, and got into the taxi she had brought.

At her house were two of her daughters, Katy and Neila. Neila was a social worker from Ealing who was visiting for Christmas. Katy worked as a nurse at a clinic. We told them the sisters' story. They told us it was similar to hundreds they had heard, and although they were very kind, they intimated, as David had done, that the mother had in all likelihood known about the marriages, and was only "screaming and shouting" now because the girls had not settled in their villages.

They told us of some other stories. "Yemen is seen as a dumping ground for kids," explained one. "Women in Britain or America marry a Yemeni. They get too many kids, so the father says he will take them home to be looked after by his parents. We had a man who came to stay recently from Britain. He brought his two-year-old son because his British wife had left him. We said to the man that he should leave the child with us, that if, as the father was planning, he took him to his village, the boy could get sick and die.

"The father said, no, his family would look after him, and he took him away. Six months later he came back. The little boy had died.

"Brides can be big business, you know. There was one British woman who married off her daughter when she was about 11. The girl became really unhappy, and wrote home, begging for help. The mother came out to Taiz, crying, and saying she would never have agreed to sell off her daughter if she had known how unhappy her baby would be. There was a lot of fuss and the woman got her daughter back, and took her home. A year later the mother sold her again, and she is living in Mokbana somewhere."

Another story concerned three sisters — aged 11, 13 and 16. They were married off by their parents in Sheffield. When the sisters arrived, it was decided the youngest was too immature for her husband. "The other two were all right. The 16-year-old insisted on a wedding ceremony, the 13-year-old accepted what had happened, though when she reached 16 she divorced her husband. This was possible because she was living with a civilised family. But the 11-year-old was a real little tomboy with punky hair. I wondered how she would get on when the boy's family decided she was old enough for the marriage bed. She had met the boy, and giggled about him being her boyfriend, not realising what the families had agreed.

"I didn't see her for about a year, and then, one day, this Yemeni girl pinched my arm when I was in the market. 'You didn't recognise me, did you?' she said, and it was the tomboy in a veil and Arab dress. She still hadn't been made to sleep with the boy, because her period hadn't started. I haven't seen her since."

The family said that some British girls married off by their parents settled well in Yemen; others were so unhappy they killed themselves. "It depends on where they are living, and what the families are like that they are married into. In Mokbana it can be very hard. The men go away to work abroad, and the wives are left with their in-laws. Lots of them just become slaves, with no status, and no one to turn to. We try to get to know about these girls and help if we can. But it can be dangerous because Mokbana is very violent, the people are very much self-governed.

"We think that just behind one of the villages where the girls you talk about are living there is an army camp. If there was to be any trouble, the army would get involved."

They told us about the Muslim Brothers, feared throughout Yemen. They are a sect of fundamentalist Muslims who are very strict with their women. Stonings for adultery are not unknown. They said Mokbana was the worst place to try to visit unhappy foreigners because of the efficiency of the mountain grapevine, and its remoteness. People literally disappeared there.

The family were willing to help, they said, but not on a wild goose chase. I emphasised my belief in the story, but could see that they were only half-convinced. Then I remembered the tape I had with me, the tape made by Zana. We put it on. It was the first time that Ben had heard it, and afterwards he said: "I had my doubts before, but they are all gone now. No one would talk like that unless it was genuine."

The family were equally moved. I had felt their mood change as the tape was playing. Neila had once started to cry, and briefly left the room. I was convinced that this family was our surest bet for getting to the girls, if only they would agree to help.

As soon as the tape was finished, the suggestions flowed thick and fast. Katy said that she thought the Director of the clinic where she worked should hear the tape because he was a representative of the Red Crescent — the Arab version of the Red Cross. He was a very caring man, she said, and would do all he could to help people in distress. He was also well-connected with important officials in Taiz, and perhaps could persuade them to act. She went on: "A couple of weeks ago the agent of the British Embassy in Taiz asked us whether we knew where the villages were. But we did not have any directions, and in Mokbana there are no signposts."

We now realised that we were with the family whom the Embassy had relied on to find the girls and bring them news of their situation. The family did not think much of the Embassy, and in particular the Vice-Consul, Mr Page, who has since been moved to Beirut. "He was very rude to everyone, never did any work, and piles of visa forms were stacked high on his desk. A real pig," was the family's verdict.

Katy said that we should come back early in the morning and she would take us to the clinic where the Director worked. "He is a kind man, and he likes to help people. If we get him on our side, things could happen quickly," she said. We left, agreeing to come back at 8.30 the next morning. On our way out, Mrs X told us that her home was sometimes watched by National Security, and that in the past her own family had been interrogated. She warned us about taxi-drivers, and was alarmed about Sultan and the way in which he had clung to us. We were glad that, although we trusted Sultan, we had paid him off earlier in the evening and he had gone.

The next morning, we breakfasted at seven. We thought it a good idea to let the Embassy know what was happening, and telephoned our diplomat. He again told us to be careful and repeated the "You could be shot" warning, coupled with a request not to endanger any other British citizen or dual national.

When we arrived at the X family home, Katy was waiting. She had to cancel an important meeting in Sana'a for us, but said she was happy to help the sisters. "We sat up talking very late after you had gone," she said. "We had never heard anything so bad as Zana's story. No one who spoke as she did could be acting. It is terrible to think of those poor girls living in that way."

We went by taxi to the clinic. It was a children's clinic, set in the heart of Taiz, and teeming with life. Whole families would accompany the sick child, sleeping around the bed, and eating makeshift meals on the floor. In the daytime, the men would gather outside to talk and chew qat.

The Director's office was on the first floor of the bright, modern building, and when we entered he was on the telephone. He waved at Katy and motioned us to sit in some comfortable chairs. When he had finished, Katy introduced us as people who had come on holiday from England, but wished to see the daughters of friends of ours who apparently were very unhappy. The Director, a silver-haired man in a white doctor's coat, seemed more European than Arabic. He was far more sophisticated than any Yemeni man we had so far met. He shook hands and said that he hoped he could help us. He launched into what was obviously his pet theme — his clinic and his plans for extensions. With only the gentlest reminder from Katy, he returned to the purpose of our visit and readily agreed to listen to the tape.

It took us an hour to play it, not because he had not meant what he said, but because the phone was constantly ringing and mothers walked in bearing sick children, sometimes with several others in tow who also benefited by a swift check-up. He talked at length on each telephone call, and took great care over each child. It became easy to understand why everything took so long in Yemen; the most pressing engagement was always being delayed by an immediate incident. As we waited Katy explained: "The mothers are not really supposed to bring the children into him, but they know he will never refuse any child, and that he is the best doctor."

An old woman, bent almost double and dressed completely in black, shuffled in with a thermos flask in her hand. She poured us coffee, which was delicious, flavoured with cinnamon. Then she brought in hot rolls filled with cheese and placed one each on our laps. Ben and I refused the food, but the Director, examining a baby with a stethoscope, seemed to become mortally offended so we smiled and ate them.

Finally, he turned to us, full of apologies, and said: "Now we listen to this story." He found a tape recorder after much fumbling in a filing cabinet, and inserted the tape. Zana's Birmingham voice filled the room. The Director frowned, got up, started pacing, then rushed out of his door. I thought that he had just remembered an urgent case, but Katy smiled, and shook her head. "He was crying," she explained. "He could not show you his tears, but he has understood."

Ten minutes later the Director came back, mopping his face with a handkerchief. He sat down on his desk and said: "I represent the Red Crescent. Do not be worried any more about these girls. This life for them will not continue. These men who have done this thing to them, their father and the boys' fathers, are filth to Yemeni people. They are animals. No, they are worse than animals, for animals look after their children.

"I know the Governor in Taiz, and today, now, I shall try to get hold of him and tell him to send his men to the girls and to bring them here to Taiz where they will be safe. Then there will be a court case and the people who have done this to them will be punished. You must tell their mother that they will be all right now. You have my word."

Part of what he had said was in Arabic, although he did his best in English, so we had understood the gist. Dramatically he snatched up the telephone on his desk, punched out a number, then had a lengthy and seemingly furious conversation. When he had finished, he spoke rapidly to Katy, who translated: "He says that the Governor is in Sana'a today, but he will get hold of him tomorrow. He is on our side," she smiled. "He says that now he has thought about it, he thinks that he has heard something of these sisters before, a few years ago. The Governor was talking about it, once, he remembers, but he did not think anything was done at the time. Now, he says, he will push it through."

It was wonderful that the Director was so moved and had promised his support and immediate action. So far, it was going much better than we had dared hope. But what we wanted was to see the girls ourselves; not rely on the Director's promise of action. I said: "We have letters and presents for the girls and their children. We promised their mother, because she is so anxious for them, that we would personally do everything we could to see the girls ourselves so that we could assure her they were all right. Would it be possible for you to arrange for us to go to the villages?" It was a pretty long shot, I thought. I was worried about pushing this man too far, and making him suspicious.

Katy translated, then interpreted what he said in reply. "He says you are very good people to do this on your holiday for your friends. He thinks there may be someone who works in the clinic who comes from one of the villages nearby originally. He will send for him."

Ten minutes later a shy youngish man in jeans and white medic's coat, appeared in the doorway. Mohammed and the Director talked at length, and I heard the names of the villages. Mohammed nodded. The Director went on, then finally turned to us, beaming. "He says he knows, and that, because I have asked him as a personal favour to help you good people, he will do it. He will miss a day's work, so you must pay him."

Ben and I could hardly believe it. We thanked the Director profusely, but he waved aside our thanks. He had another rapid conversation with Katy. She told us: "He is very worried about your safety in Mokbana. He says you must be very careful and do everything that Mohammed tells you, because he knows the ways of the men there. He says that if you are not back by six o'clock this evening, he will telephone the police to rescue you, so you must not be afraid if anything happens, because it will not last long."

I thought it was going to be difficult to do everything that Mohammed told us because he spoke no English and we spoke no Arabic. But we could always follow his gestures — like "duck" and "put your hands up".

Mohammed took us outside to the hospital yard. There stood a gleaming, white brand new jeep, with the green UNICEF symbol on the door. He grinned, pulled open a door, and helped us in. Katy was delighted. "This will make it much easier," she said. "The villagers throughout Mokbana know this jeep and Mohammed. It brings medicines and supplies the little clinic right in the middle of Mokbana. There has never been any trouble or shooting for the people in this jeep."

We took Katy home first, so that she could rearrange her meeting and get to Sana'a later in the day. Inside the house, Neila appeared with her mother, wanting to know everything that had happened. They too were delighted. "You are very lucky, everything is going to be all right," said Mrs X.

Neila said: "I know you are going to make it, I feel it, and when I feel something in advance it always happens. The only thing is, can I come too?"

Ben and I readily agreed. Neila was fluent in English, unlike her sister who had lived in Yemen all her life and spoke it rather hesitantly with a Cardiff accent. Neila also knew Mohammed, and would be able to interpret the "Duck!" command. We were to be very grateful to Neila at the end of the day. I think she saved our necks on at least two occasions.

The only problem we faced with an extra passenger was seating. But that was easily resolved. Neila and I would sit up in front with Mohammed. As there was only seating for three, Ben would go in the back, on the ice-box. Mrs X was busily filling it with ice so that we could stop on the way and buy soft drinks. Ben did not look over-enamoured at the prospect. Katy, kinder than Neila and I, suggested the garden chair, so it was set up in the back for Ben. Unfortunately, about 20 minutes out of Taiz, there was a loud ripping noise, then a bang. Ben had broken the chair,

Nadia and Zana with the children, February 1988.

and had landed uncomfortably on the jeep's floor, so in the end it was the ice-box.

Neila provided me with a head-dress, not out of modesty, she explained, but because of the heat and the dust which was always bad in Mokbana.

It was about 11 o'clock in the morning. By two that afternoon, all being well — "Ensha Allah", God willing, in Arabic — we should be with the Muhsen girls.

Chapter Eleven

Our first stop had to be the petrol station in Taiz, at which there were long queues. "In a country which has just discovered oil, you would think they could spare some for the engines," said Neila.

Her presence had boosted our morale enormously. Suddenly we felt more as if we were going for a picnic in Mokbana than a foray into enemy territory. Neila had been to Mokbana several times before with her friends, almost for a day out in the country, she told us. I felt it was probably going to be easy, that the various warnings had just been scare stories. Then Neila told us: "Of course we always had our guns."

Mohammed, beside me, laughed. "He says you look scared," said Neila. Probably to reassure me, Mohammed reached down under his seat and produced his own gun, a Luger pistol — loaded. He handed it to me, saying: "Bang, bang." I turned to show it to Ben, who took a dive on to the floor. Little trust did he have in me. I needed him alive for the photographs.

The atmosphere in our jeep was becoming increasingly like a school-outing; we were all very excited. Mohammed, in his absolute innocence about his two passengers, was our greatest security, I thought. If anyone did stop us he would truthfully say we were just tourists visiting friends.

We stopped a short distance from Taiz to buy drinks and sweets for the village children. "Always take presents for the children," Neila told us. We stocked up with her favourite drink, banana milk shake, ten bottles of water and cans of pepsi-cola. We were out on the open road now, German-built, straight and smooth. We passed through a small town, at the end of which Mohammed stopped, went into a shop and came out carrying opium seeds, which he offered us to chew. Neila prompted us to take some, saying they had no effect, but we were wary. The last thing we wanted to be when we rolled up to the villages was stoned.

There was yet another stop for Mohammed to check the tyres and hose down the jeep to keep it cool. As he did so, a lorry with an entire family inside and spilling out, hanging to its edges, pulled up. The woman called to Neila and waved qat at her. We decided to buy vast quantities, both for Mohammed and Neila, but also for the villagers. "It will give them something to chew on," said Neila.

Off we went again with the dashboard of the UNICEF jeep now resembling an alternative drugs counter of poppy seeds and qat branches. Neila, sitting beside me wearing her head-dress and sunglasses, looked like a peaceful terrorist as she chewed her qat leaves. She tried to teach me some Arabic. She told me that "Mafish moch" meant nutty, literally, "no brains". I used it on Mohammed as he squealed round a corner on the road; he was delighted. He and Neila talked, then she translated: "He says he cannot understand your parents allowing you to come to this country, even with your husband, and to go off with strangers. It is the Yemeni culture. No woman, no matter what her age, would be allowed here to go out for the day to Mokbana, or anywhere else for that matter, with people who were not close friends of the family.

"He thinks it is very strange too for me to be with you. He knows that we have only just met. He says it must be because we have British blood."

I told Neila about the warnings which we had received. "No they won't shoot us — probably," she laughed. "We have got our guns too, remember. A lot of the mountain men like to shout and wave their guns around, but when we have been to Mokbana before, just showing that you have got your gun usually cools them down. We can always shoot back."

Mohammed had been fiddling with the jeep's cassette player. Suddenly it burst into life, playing *I shot the sheriff*. We joined in, singing: "We shot the sheyekh". Mohammed, having arrived at the conclusion that we were all mad, sang too, not understanding a word.

About an hour out of Taiz, we passed a small settlement on the right hand side of the road. Mohammed swung the jeep up a narrow alleyway, and we bounced and jogged along the unmade track. After a while, the track opened out on to wasteland, and we kept going, crossing a river, which was the start of Mokbana. The road had now vanished, and it was becoming a very bumpy ride, with rocks and boulders strewn in our path.

The start of Mokbana was beautiful, as we drove along beside the river — very green, with palm trees and kingfishers. Then the mountains began in earnest, and the land was dry and barren.

The jeep leapt and crashed down on to the ground again. In the front we were flung around; in the back Ben was moaning softly on the floor. Mohammed laughed and Neila said: "We haven't even started yet."

She was right. The jeep was now crawling along at five miles per hour, screaming as we started to ascend our first mountain. Neila said that taxis went into Mokbana; I thought their suspensions must be in shreds.

Up and down, round and over the mountains we went. Far below us we saw the valleys, with rough-hewn fields. Once we passed a gypsy encampment of tents made with animal hide. Camels were tethered to a nearby tree. "They are the nomad people," Neila explained. "They wander through Mokbana, and work sometimes in the towns, doing the street-cleaning. Their women are tough, and uncovered. Their men send the women to markets to sell cloth and to barter. They are the only women you will see uncovered. They wear beautiful gold jewellery and bright dresses."

Neila, largely fearless, was terrified of heights. She clung on desperately as we crawled up a particularly high incline, her eyes shut tight at the sheer drop just a couple of feet on our right hand side. "I think I am going to faint," she said repeatedly, but never did.

On one such stretch, when we had hit the ceiling of the truck several times, I thought that I really must get hold of something that was solid enough to stop me leaving the seat. I searched around underneath the seat. My fingers touched and enclosed metal. Pleased, I clung on. The next twenty minutes I remained firmly sitting while Neila bounced around. Then I looked under the seat. I was clutching the barrel of a gun. I dropped it very quickly.

We started entering villages. Everyone came out to see us, but they were waving with their hands not their guns. "See, no road-blocks, no one is shooting us," said Neila. "I don't know what David was talking about when he said the villagers would be out with guns. They would only do that if they knew who you were and what you had come for." She leaned out of the window to give some children sweets. Mohammed was engaged in conversation as we bounced along. Neila said: "Everyone is asking for medicines. Everyone knows him and the jeep, and they need supplies. They can't understand why we are not stopping to distribute, but Mohammed has said the drugs we have are for the clinic further on. I hope there is no trouble."

Mohammed stopped the jeep and got out to talk to a group of men, many with machine-guns on show. There was shouting like gunfire, much arm-waving. Then he got in, grinning, and we were off again. He was laughing and talking to Neila. She said: "He said that you and Ben are doctors from England, and you have come to see two sick friends. You are Doctor Ben and you are Doctor Eileen, all the way from England."

"I hope no one asks us to do an operation," said Ben from the back.

Another agonising few miles, and then we pulled up again, this time outside what appeared to be a school or hospital. Mohammed left us and came back with a young man. Neila said that Mohammed did not know where the villages were exactly, and he hoped this man could tell him. We drank banana milk-shakes while the route was being discussed. Suddenly the other man leaned into the truck and said to me in perfect English: "I had an English wife but she left me."

I was so taken aback that I just said: "Oh well, these things happen." He nodded sadly and walked away.

We bumped on again. Like children, Ben and I kept asking: "How much longer, Neila?" and Neila said, conferring with Mohammed: "Not far." I had the crazy thought that as we edged along the track we would see coming towards us a jeep marked *Sunday Mirror* with the girls and their children waving at us, on their way home.

When we did run into a jeep, however, it proved to be a very friendly man, who said that he knew where the villages were and would take us. "Is he safe?" I asked, fearing he could be a scout from Hockail.

"I think so," said Neila.

The man took us many miles out of his way, then at a tiny village, stopped and talked to Mohammed. Neila told us that our guide said that he would have to leave us, but that he was first going to the school in another village to bring back a boy from Ashube, so that he could travel with us and direct us.

It showed how remote the villages were. We were, at this point, only about 20 minutes from the girls, but inhabitants of the mountain living so nearby did not know where the villages were.

True to his word, the man left and returned with a young boy, who climbed into the back of the jeep beside Ben. He stood up on the ice-box and shouted instructions to Mohammed. Neila talked to him, and translated to us. "I asked him if he knew the homes of Nadia and Zana, and he says, 'Oh yes. Nadia lives in the house on the mountain with the yellow door.'" Ben and I cheered.

We started to grind our way up our last mountain. It was Mountain Ala Sharub, the boy said. Right at the top was a small village, its houses clinging on to the rockface. "Ashube," said the boy. Then he pointed to a house, whitewashed, with yellow painted windows and doors. "Nadia," he said.

It was like a magic password. Somehow I couldn't believe we were actually going to see the girls; after what we had heard they had become merely characters in a play. The boy was talking again to Neila. She said: "He says they are called the poor, sad sisters of Mokbana. They are always crying, he says. They want to go home, but the men say they never will."

The girls had not been moved. This was Miriam's fear. She knew that communication with the fathers-in-law and the villages was good, and that there was no doubt that press stories in Britain about them would now have reached the villages.

Mountain Ala Sharub was proving too much for our jeep. About half way up the stone track stopped and it was rockface. We got out of the jeep, Ben with his cameras, the rest of us laden with bottles of water and sweets. Ben gave me a camera because it looked less suspicious than his being laden with two. I was also carrying presents for the girls and the children.

With the sun blazing down — it was 2.30 p.m. — we clambered up the mountain. The boy, of course, ran ahead. Looking straight up I saw that at the top a woman was waiting for us. As each of us reached her, she embraced us. The boy had told the woman, who lived in Ashube, that we were from England, doctors and friends to see the sisters. The children of Ashube had come to stare at the foreigners, so we distributed sweets. "Where are the girls?" I asked Neila. "The woman says that they are in the other village, in Hockail. Their brother from the army is with them. They are allowed to be together because he is there."

The woman was pulling us into her house — Nadia's was another short climb up the mountain. She was smiling and touching my hair. "Don't leave anything behind when you leave her house," warned Neila. "Don't leave your bag on the floor, she will go through it."

We ducked as we went into the woman's house. Inside it was very dark, made of stone, with tiny windows. She motioned us to the mattresses on the floor, and we sat down. She told Neila that the boy had been sent running for the sisters. We could not get to Hockail by jeep, there was no road, but the boy would be back in 20 minutes.

The woman brought us a plastic beaker, and a jug of water. "Don't drink the water," said Neila, producing our own bottles. The woman did not seem offended. She picked up the jug, shrugged at the water, which she had probably carried some distance from the well on her head, and threw it outside. She had covered her face with a veil, holding an edge of it in her teeth. She squatted on the floor and talked. "Oh, no," said Neila suddenly. "She has told the boy that I am the girls' mother, and that is what he will tell them. She says she met me before when I came. I don't think much of her eyesight."

I dreaded what the disappointment of the sisters would be when they arrived and found strangers.

The woman, through Neila, said: "Have you come to take them home? They will want to go with you. You should take them home. They are very unhappy. But they will have to leave the children here and there is no one to look after them."

The boy bounded back into the room. He was shouting. "They are coming," said Neila, and went outside, with us following. Running up the mountain were two Arab women. One clutched a baby and a little boy ran crying at her side. The other woman was alone and running faster. When they reached our little group, they stopped, gasping. Then without a word, they ran on up the mountain and disappeared into the house we knew as Nadia's, the one with the yellow door. "They are very shocked," said Neila. "We must leave them a little while."

Waiting was agony. Suppose the distress and disappointment meant that the girls would not see us? We stood helplessly for a few minutes, then a child came out of Nadia's house and beckoned us. We went up to the door, and an elderly woman opened it cautiously.

Inside we were led up stone stairs, then across a landing into a bright room that ran the width of the house. There seemed to be a lot of people sitting on the mattresses. A very old man, four younger ones, and various women. At the far end of the room sat one of the girls who had run past. She looked small, dressed completely in black, with a head-dress covering her face. Beside her was a young man, looking very frightened.

I walked slowly over to the girl, noticing that the conversation in the room had stopped. When I reached her, she looked up, unsmiling. "I am Zana," she said. She was trembling, and sweating. Her eyes were fixed to my face.

I shook her hand and said: "Hello, Zana. I am Eileen. I know your mother, and we have come to talk to you." We had decided that we could not say immediately that we were journalists, because we did not know who understood English in the village.

Zana said: "Aren't you Geraldine? Mum said it was Geraldine who would come."

At first I was confused, then remembered that Zana must be talking about Geraldine Van Bueren, of Defence of Children International. Zana went on, speaking low: "You have come to take us away, haven't you? We have been waiting ever since Mum left for you to come. We have waited 20 months. We can't wait no more."

The room was deathly quiet. I said: "Be careful, Zana. We will talk later. Where is Nadia?"

Zana pointed to a girl in a black and yellow dress sitting on a shelf beside a window. She seemed very remote. "That's my sister," said Zana.

I took Nadia's hand and said hello. She raised her eyes. They were dead. "Have you come to take us away?" she asked.

I wanted to say, yes, get into the jeep, but I could not. The men in the room were talking to Neila and Mohammed. Mohammed was on his feet, with his pistol stuffed into his trousers at the waist, clearly visible. He fingered it as he talked.

"This is my brother, Ahmed," said Zana, touching the arm of the young man beside her. "We didn't know we had a brother until Mum came. He is visiting us. Last week he arrived with a car. He said he had come for us, because he knew how unhappy we were. He said to put the children in the back of the car and he would take us out of here, to a safe place. But me and Nadia said no because our mum had told us to wait until help came. We knew our mum would send help to us. We are glad we waited now for you because now we will go with you and everything will be all right."

Ahmed nervously smiled at me, not understanding a word. Zana translated into Arabic, and he nodded, and smiled again, looking as if a load was off his shoulders. This was awful, I thought. We had not planned to rescue the girls, only to talk to them.

Neila and Mohammed were now shouting, and so was the rest of the room. Neila came over and said to me: "This could get very nasty. They suspect you are journalists. They know that newspapers have written about the girls, and someone has called a man in another village to say that people are coming to get the girls. I have told them that you are doctors with presents for the girls from their mothers. I don't know if they believe us. Can you go outside for a bit?"

Ben, who had been at the other end of the room, trying to understand what was going on, came over too. I asked Zana if we could go outside for a walk and to talk. She and Nadia rose, Nadia picking up her baby girl. Shouting from the men, shouting from the girls. Then Zana said to me: "Come on. I have said you are not going to kidnap us. We will show you the village."

It was about this time, half past three in the afternoon, when

Gohad Abdul Majid, Nadia's father-in-law living in Willows Road, Birmingham telephoned Taiz. He spoke to the commander of the villages, who was also in charge of his own police force. He said that he had just heard that two journalists were in Yemen, looking for the girls. They were dangerous, and they were spies, said Gohad. They would cause great trouble for Yemen. The commander promised immediate action, and slammed down the receiver.

Ashube, December 1987.

Chapter Twelve

Zana led Ben and me out of the house, with Nadia following, still holding her baby. "We have to go away to talk, otherwise one of them that speaks English will come and sit with us," said Zana.

We followed her down the mountain to another house. There, squatting in true Yemeni style, between the house wall and the mountain edge, Nadia spoke for the first time. The Birmingham idiom "yous" for you was still in both girls' speech, but even more startling from Nadia, because she appeared the picture of Yemeni womanhood. Nursing her daughter, Tina, aged 22 months, she said: "Yous is from that place in Switzerland, aren't yous? That place Mum talked about that was trying to get us out."

I said that no, I was not from Defence of Children, but a journalist from a newspaper in London called *The Observer*. "I remember that one," said Zana. "I read it sometimes at home. But yous have come to take us, haven't you?"

I said that we did not think we could take them that afternoon, because we only had one jeep, and that a UNICEF one. It would be risking all of us to go without papers for the girls and the children. They would only be sent back. "Ahmed has got a car," said Nadia.

Ben and I thought about this. Maybe it would be possible to arrange something. "We will talk about it to Neila," we promised. We were both very aware that at any moment our time with the sisters might be interrupted by village men. I asked the girls when they had last seen their husbands and whether they were around at the moment.

"Them," Zana spat out her hatred. "We haven't seen them for two years. They're both in Saudi, thank God."

Nadia, deadpan, added: "We cannot accept them. They beat us."

I asked the girls if they could tell me their story, in their own words, from the beginning. They looked blank. "What do you mean?" asked Zana. I asked them just to describe their life. It was obviously very difficult for them. It seemed as if they could not find the words.

Zana sighed, and began: "Well, I was going to be a nursery nurse and I had just left school. Dad was very strict with us. He wouldn't let us go out. We wasn't allowed to go to discos. We was never allowed to have boyfriends. He used to hit us. Then he said me and Nadia could come on a holiday. We was really excited but when I got here I was married to this boy, he was smaller than me. They said they was going to hold me down so I slept with him.

"There was no marriage, nothing. We are like slaves here and my family hates me. They beat me, but I say I'm going home. It's much worse since our mum came. Now they don't trust us. They watch us all the time. Mum said not to tell them nothing, but I couldn't help it. It was the only way I could go on, telling them I was going home and they'd be sorry for what they'd done.

"We are scared of them, you know. I was up at Nadia's the other week, in the evening, and we was crying. She was worse than me 'cos she's got the other kids to look after 'cos that Gohad's wife has gone to England and left them with her. She was only meant to be gone three months for medical treatment, and she's been gone nearly two years. Nadia writes letters to her saying she can't cope with her two kids, they're horrible, they bite her, and asking her to come back and get them. But she never answers the letters. She don't care about her kids. Why should she, 'cos she knows Nadia is here in hell looking after them? Anyway, I'd stayed on to help with them kids, and it got late, later than I should have been back at my house, so I ran in the dark. And when I got home, this uncle of mine, he hit me, hard. He said I was evil, I was sleeping with other men in the village. I said I was never, but he didn't believe me. He likes hitting me.

"My mother-in-law hates me most of them all. Nadia's lot treat her all right. They are sorry for her with her two and those other kids. My mother-in-law tells the men stories that are lies about what I am like, then they hit me. She does it deliberately and she smiles when they hit me.

"They said that if we try to get away, they will send the men with the guns for us. There's an army camp just over the mountain, you know. We would never·go,'cos we don't know the way and we'd die. We'd have to take the kids, or Nadia would have to take hers, 'cos she won't leave them. I'd leave mine. He's up at the house now. I'd leave mine, I could go with yous back home."

Nadia broke in, but in Arabic. The girls talked.

"I wouldn't leave mine unless I had to," Zana continued. "Not in hell, in nothing here. Look at the way the kids live here, they've got nothing."

A small group of children, among them Nadia's four-year-old son, Haney, had gathered at the end of the house. They were all under six, and were scrambling up and down the rock face. One or two had simple sandals, the rest were bare-footed.

"They don't have toys, you know," said Zana. "They don't have nothing. When the husbands come home, I mean, they're not our husbands, but that's what you've got to call them, they don't want to sleep with us, but they make them, the other men here. Then they laugh about it. My husband, he got me pregnant once, but now I don't let him have me, not if I can help it. I sleep away from him, or if he makes me, I just lie there and let him get on with it. He knows I hate him, so he doesn't try much. I wish I could get on the pill, but they'd kill me if they found out. They say I'm no good anyway 'cos I haven't had lots of kids. I hope the one I'm married to divorces me or just gets another wife."

I was sitting opposite the girls, squatting like them. Ben was moving around us, taking pictures. Nadia, unsmiling, stared into the lens. She reminded me of someone in shock; she was so withdrawn. She often started speaking in Arabic, then stopped herself and slowly spoke in English.

"I went to have my tonsils out in Taiz a week ago," she said. "It was the first time in a long time we had been out of here. But they never leave us alone. They think we are going to escape."

I asked her if she ever felt, like Zana, that she would leave her children behind to get out. She gazed down at her daughter on her breast. "Well, it's not their fault they're here, is it? If I was to leave them, I'd be scared they'd die, 'cos no one else would care for them. We was forced into bed with their fathers, and I hate him just as much as Zana hates hers, but I wouldn't want to take it out on the kids. Not leave them here, to what happened to us. You wouldn't believe it.

"When I got here and they said I was married to him and they dragged me off to the room, he didn't want to do it. He was only 13. Then one night Gohad came and pulled me into the room. He locked me in. Then I heard him outside shouting at his son, then he started to beat him really bad. The boy was screaming and screaming, it was terrible. Then Gohad unlocked the door and flung him in. I will never forget it, that night."

At first, said the sisters, they believed their mother was in league with their father in selling them as brides. Zana said: "When we was being shown how to make the chapatis by putting our hands in the fire, and we got burned, I remember thinking they would burn in hell for what they done to us. I couldn't believe my father had done what he had. Selling us for £1,300 each, like we was cattle. Then when we knew our mum had done nothing, and all the suffering she was having with us and trying to get us back, we knew our mum could never have been in on it. She always loved us. She was always there. I was ashamed of what I'd thought of her, but how was we to know the truth? I can't tell you what I'd like to do to my father. I want him to die slowly, like what we have been doing. I want him to suffer and I wouldn't be sorry. I'd spit on him, and on his grave."

They told us of the hard life and constant work they had, only relieved when they got a letter from home. I asked if they could still remember Birmingham. Zana was scornful: "Of course we can. The little houses, and all those people, everyone free. You know what I miss most? The rain."

They told me of having to make the "happy" tape for their father. "It broke my heart," said Zana. "I thought when I was making it and writing those happy letters and having to sound cheerful that no one would ever find us. I thought no one would know what was really going on; they'd believe we was happy. I hoped if people that knew us ever heard it, they would know I wouldn't talk that way. I could not tell the truth 'cos the men were right behind us, and they'd got Nadia. But I knew our father would never play it to anyone who cared about us."

They said that Ben and I were lucky to have arrived on that particular day, because normally they were not allowed to be

Nadia and Tina, December 1987.

together. "It's only 'cos Ahmed's here," said Zana. "Ahmed loves us and he cried when he heard what had happened. I remember Mum telling us that we had a brother and an older sister Leila but our father had taken them away to Yemen and they was meant to be happy. Ahmed never was. He was beaten for years by our grandfather in Marais. Then, when he went into the army and started to travel around, he heard about us, and he found us last year. He comes to see us when he can, but he can't very often because he has to get leave. The men here don't trust him, they know he loves us and wants to take us away somewhere where we'll be happy. But they have to let him see us, 'cos he's our brother."

We had moved by this stage on to a rockface, so that Ben could take photographs. It was out in the direct, harsh sunlight. Touchingly, Zana said to us as she and her sister squatted on the rock: "Yous two better be careful in the sun. We're all right; we're used to it."

We had been there only five minutes when, looking below, we saw an old man with white hair and beard, toiling up the mountain towards us. "It's that old bastard," said Zana to her sister. Then to us: "He's come to spy on us. It don't matter what he says, he's nothing. He understands English good, though."

The old man sat beside Ben and started engaging him in conversation. Ben said that we were doctors and he had a keen interest in photography, and that the pictures of the girls were for their mother. I had put my notebook away. I went over to the old man whom Zana was shouting at in Arabic. He was shouting back. He said to Ben and me: "I know England good. I come from Sheffield. The girls are happy here, you tell their mother. They don't cause trouble."

His presence made it impossible for us to carry on with the interview.

As we were climbing the mountain, back towards Nadia's house, she said: "So we can come with you, then?"

Thinking about the other car that their brother had, I said: "We can talk to your brother about it. But it will be risky."

"So's being here," said Zana.

The old man walked in front of us as we reached the house. Back in the upstairs room of Nadia's home, the number of men had grown. There was not only the old man from Sheffield, but two others who seemed to be particularly suspicious of us.

The girls led us over to where their brother was and talked to him. He nodded and smiled again at Ben and me. Neila detached herself from Mohammed and the men and sat beside me. "We are going to have to be very careful here," she said. "The old man says you are journalists because he saw your notebook, and Ben's cameras. Those two younger ones (she jerked her head at the two I had noticed) are nasty and spoiling for action."

I told Neila of the girls' suggestion that their brother could take them out in his car. Neila called over Mohammed, and they talked for some time, very quietly. There we were, the escape party in one corner, and the increasingly suspicious men in the other.

Neila told us: "Mohammed has heard the girls' story now from the brother. He wants to help, but he can't take them in the jeep. Not with UNICEF on it, and him so well known in Mokbana. But if Ahmed has got another car, what is to stop him taking his sisters and their children into Taiz to stay with friends? We could all go out together." She turned to the girls: "Don't talk, just get the kids ready. No luggage."

Zana and Nadia needed no further prompting. They both rose, Nadia collecting her two children, and left us. They came back with food, tuna from a tin, it tasted like, and bread. We joined the men and ate it. Neila kept telling me they were very uptight, we had to act like tourists. Ben and I did the best we could with the language barrier, smiling and nodding, talking loudly about the seaside.

Then the girls were back with the children, all dressed up for a journey. Everyone was suddenly on their feet. Mohammed talked to Ahmed, with his hand on his gun. The younger men were all standing, one hanging on to Zana's arm. The old man sat regally, directing the proceedings. The shouting lasted for some time, with Neila suggesting someone get our qat. The girls came over and sat beside me. Mohammed and Neila joined us. Mohammed talked earnestly to the girls, then Neila, who finally translated. "The brother hasn't got his car with him today. There is no way we can do it in the jeep." Turning to the girls, she said: "We can't do it today, but your brother says he wants to bring back some of his army friends tomorrow and take you with the kids. You will have to wait."

A small contingent of the army might just do it, I thought, but it also might end in blood.

The qat was produced, and things quietened down. The girls were very upset. Suddenly the old man shouted out in English : "Take the girls, and leave the children."

Zana was prepared to do so; Nadia was not.

After a while the sisters cleared up the plates and left. We talked on with Ahmed, using Neila as our interpreter. She said: "These men here, they really seem to like the girls, they don't want them to go. They are also very guilty, trying to cover up for what's happened. They keep saying they've done nothing wrong. Ahmed says he knows how sad his sisters are and what has happened to them. He wants to come tomorrow afternoon with soldiers to get them. I think we should take him back to see the Director of the clinic, who can introduce him to the Governor of Taiz, so that he can plead on his sisters' behalf. I don't know about his plan to bring in the army. It could be dangerous."

It was at this point that Nadia came back into the room, and led me to another where Zana was crying. I told her about her brother's plan and she perked up. I said that even if he did not come back with soldiers the next day, he would come back with news. He was going to try to see the Governor, and Ben and I were going to do a report as soon as we got back. We would also be seeing the Embassy. "Please be patient a little longer," I said. "Things will happen soon, I promise you that."

They both seemed slightly more cheerful. Zana suggested her plan of getting into Taiz by saying that their mother was there and sick. But the old man from Sheffield scuppered that route of escape by insisting first that one of the villagers see the mother before the girls would be allowed to leave.

It was a very desperate scene in that room. Zana, still trying not to cry, was sitting on a wooden trunk. Nadia seemed stronger at that moment. "We know yous are going to help us," she said. "It's just we have been waiting so long, and we thought we was going to leave now. But we can be patient some more time."

I went back into the other room with the girls. Neila called them over and said very quietly in English: "You must not say anything about tomorrow. When you were whispering to your brother earlier on, I was at the other end of the room and I could hear every word you were saying. They are already very suspicious. You don't want them moving you away, or locking you up somewhere, do you?"

The girls shrugged. "They can't stop us talking," said Zana defiantly.

"I don't know," I replied. "But I hope things will have happened before then."

Neila said: "If we can get the Director to arrange a meeting tomorrow with Ahmed, and you can talk to him too, then things could move very quickly. It all depends on the Governor and what view he takes of it. Ahmed could help a lot if he gets the Governor on his side."

She told the girls that, as Yemeni wives, they were free to go into Taiz as often as they liked. The girls looked very disbelieving. Nadia said: "They don't let us go nowhere. We are prisoners here. We are not like you or normal Yemeni women. They keep us here as if we had chains on."

There was nothing more we could do in the villages for the girls, so we picked up the cameras, and a much dwindled supply of qat, and started down to our jeep. We shook hands with the girls before we left. "You won't forget us, will yous?" they said.

Ahmed joined Ben in the back of the jeep, sharing the ice-box. We had two skirmishes on our way out of Mokbana. Once, a jeep blocked our path and armed men circled our Land Rover, searching for the girls. A little further on, an entire village came out to inspect our passengers, just in case the sisters were with us. On both occasions Neila and Mohammed managed to extricate us. We made it back to Taiz in three hours. Mohammed said, through Neila, "The villages are 12 miles into Mokbana. It takes two and a half hours to get there because of the track."

Ahmed was largely silent on the journey to Taiz. Once or twice Neila and Mohammed tried to engage him in talking, but he was monosyllabic. "He is boiling up to do something that could get everyone killed," said Neila. "I think we are going to have to have a long talk with him tonight."

Chapter Thirteen

When we reached Taiz, in the early evening, Ahmed asked Mohammed to leave him at a car-hire depot. He wanted to drive through the night to Marais, pick up his army identification papers and collect his soldier friends. "He wants to go back at first light and get the girls out," said Neila. "We have to persuade him not to do it."

Much against his will, and with a great deal of shouting, Ahmed came back to Neila's home. The house was packed with friends visiting the family and Neila and her mother ushered us all into a back room. "We don't know if we can trust them, and anyway, it's better for them that they don't know what is going on," said Mrs X.

Ahmed sat miserably on the floor, refusing to eat or drink. "He says he wants nothing until his sisters are out of Mokbana," said Neila. "He says that his sisters are relying on him, and he has told them to be waiting from dawn tomorrow. It could all go horribly wrong."

Her mother joined in the argument with Ahmed. Finally, looking defeated, he nodded his head. We agreed that early in the morning we would take him with us to see the Director of the clinic. Afterwards, Ahmed insisted, he would return to the villages to bring his sisters to Taiz.

Neila telephoned the Director to assure him we were all safe and arranged the meeting. He was on the point of calling out the police, she told us.

We did not know until a month after we had returned from North Yemen that the police chief was already well aware of our presence. For some reason, he did not send out a squad to Mokbana that afternoon. He delayed until the following morning at dawn, when, of course, it was too late. The villagers told them we had been and gone. If Gohad had made his call a day earlier, we would have walked into an ambush. But we were now being looked for by the police, a fact of which we were blissfully unaware.

We decided that if Ahmed did manage to bring the girls out, we would drive through the night with them straight to the British Embassy. Ben and I would have to travel in a separate car, because Yemeni women and Westerners travelling together would arouse suspicion at the road-blocks. The girls, and their children, would have no papers but the family considered it was possible the soldiers on road-block duty would ask no questions once they saw their brother's army documentation. They could simply say it was a family trip to visit relatives in Sana'a.

To have stayed in Taiz, everyone thought, would be dangerous. The villagers had many relatives living in the town, and they could very quickly report back. We thought that, once at the Embassy, the girls' plight could be sorted out much more easily than trying to negotiate in Mokbana.

I telephoned the British diplomat and told him of our news. He sounded amazed, but delighted. I said that it was just possible that the girls and their children would be coming to Sana'a the next day, if their brother's attempt to fetch them the following evening was successful. He said: "Fine, we will arrange some beds. Be careful, though. You are not home yet." His warning was repeated by Robin Lustig at *The Observer* office, who said: "Don't get cocky and don't speak so much on the phone. You never know who is listening."

We went over Ahmed's plan again and again. He was to say that he was simply taking the girls to Taiz. We resurrected their sick mother story, and began to wonder if, after all, it might be possible to bring Miriam out to Taiz. Neila and her family conferred. They said they knew people who would let Miriam have a bed in a hospital, and they could arrange to make her look ill, possibly even attach a drip. I telephoned *The Observer* in London again, and we were given the go-ahead. It all depended, though, on the girls being allowed to leave the following day. We could not fly Miriam out on a no-hoper; it would be too cruel. Then we looked speculatively at Mrs X; she was about Miriam's age. We decided she could be a substitute Miriam if the girls would only be allowed to leave once a villager had seen the sick mother.

Mrs X, a lady of enormous guts and spirit, agreed. It was a crazy plan, but it might just work. "Crazy things work here," said Mrs X. "Take the girls' story, for instance. They have been kidnapped and kept like prisoners for seven years, yet until you came no one knew about it."

She had been very moved by our description of events that afternoon, shaking her head over how the girls were forced to sleep with the boys. "It is against Muslim law," she said. "A girl is supposed to be asked three times whether she wants her husband, at the marriage ceremony. But in most cases, in Yemen, this doesn't happen. Not with the first marriage. By the time the girl has divorced and remarried she knows the score, but at her first marriage, she is likely to be 12 or 13 years old, and her parents don't tell her. I have seen girls of nine and ten dragged screaming into a hut where their husband is waiting. What a way to end your childhood."

We talked on for hours, Ahmed recalling his childhood in Marais, with Neila translating. "He can't remember his life in England, and doesn't speak a word of English," she said. "His grandfather brought him up, but because he hated Muthana, he used to take it out on Ahmed. He was beaten constantly, and now his grandfather won't allow him to marry. It is a terrible thing to do to a man in Yemen, the worst. His grandfather must really hate him."

She said that Ahmed had also been taunted by the village children who used to say that he had a Christian mother. "They used to say that about us, too," said Neila. "We were called whities by the Yemeni kids, so we used to fight them."

She said that the sisters had in fact good homes by Yemeni standards. She drew our attention to the various signs of comfort that the sisters enjoyed — for instance, the pretty, painted cups in which we had been served tea. Apparently, in Yemen, many households have just one plastic beaker for drinking, and that is usually reserved for guests — for instance, that was the case in the first house we had been ushered into. Neila also commented that the girls' clothes were good quality, and that Nadia's home had been freshly decorated and boasted proper floors with linoleum laid down instead of mud or cement.

"If they had been brought up here, they would probably be quite content. The trouble is, of course, that they were tricked into their marriages and they were British through and through at 14 and 15. They have also been brainwashed and they are scared out of their wits. If we had known about them we could have visited them. If they had not been so scared they could have come up with dozens of excuses for bringing the children into Taiz — like having their inoculations. Or one of the sisters could have said she was sick. Yemeni wives often come to Taiz for a party. But those villagers have made the girls believe it's the Middle Ages in Yemen."

Her mother interrupted: "Yemen is like a police state in lots of ways. All this fear of the National Security Police, and it being dangerous to talk to foreigners. My son was arrested and held in their prison because they said that he was a member of the University's student movement that was against the Government. He did not even know about the movement, far less was he a member of it. But they locked him up and said they would break every bone in his body. He saw it being done to other people in the prison. Every evening they would come and drag some poor soul out of his cell and dip him in the sewage lake in the middle of the prison yard. They forced my son to sign his own death warrant, to confess that he had plotted to overthrow the authorities. But I got on to all the right people, shouting and screaming, and they got my son out.

"As long as you know the right people, it is not such a bad place. You have to be very careful, though, not to offend, and the trouble is that they don't tell you that you are doing something wrong, they arrest you for it."

She told us about a friend of theirs, a priest, who had worked in Taiz, ministering to a convent. He had for some reason fallen foul of the authorities, and they were looking for an excuse to deport him. One day he was down at Mokha, by the harbour, taking photographs. He was suddenly picked up by National Security for spying and bundled into a truck. At his interrogation, he was accused of being a spy because he was taking pictures in a military zone, although there was no notice to warn the casual photographer, and no sign of military activity. With this total lack of guidelines, tourists were deported sometimes without ever knowing the reason why.

"But there are some things they do right here," she continued. "There were two men recently executed in public for raping two little girls. It was televised. They showed the court case, with the men sitting there out of their minds chewing qat. When the sentence was passed, and they were taken to where they were going to be shot, they whipped them first, but only very lightly because they were going to be killed. Then they shot them. Not very well, with Kalashnikovs — the bullets went everywhere. But I don't think they felt a thing with all the qat. I think it was good that rapists get executed."

Ben and I left late, utterly exhausted. The next morning we were back at the house early, collected Neila and Ahmed, and went to the clinic. On the way we finally discarded the sick mother plan; it was too involved, and put too many people at risk. We decided to trust the Director of the clinic.

This time, when we knocked on his door, the Director was waiting for us, and mothers with children were kept waiting outside.

Ahmed told the story of his sisters, and we chimed in with how unhappy and desperate they were. The Director tried again to contact the Governor of Taiz, Muhsen Al Usifi, but was told that he was still in Sana'a. He turned to Ben and me. Speaking partially through Neila, he said: "The Governor will be told of this by me as soon as he returns to Taiz. I promise you that. The girls will be brought into Taiz to be asked questions. If the Governor wishes it, then they can go home to their mother at once. If he wants to hear the husbands' side, then they will be recalled to Taiz from Saudi Arabia and there will be a court case. The girls must ask for divorce. It will cost lots of money and could take five years. Everyone has to be bribed — from the soldiers who go into Mokbana to fetch them, they will want 12,000 rials each, to the lawyers, and the judges."

It was quite an insight into the corruption of the society. The Director said he thought that he knew the sheyekh of the area where the girls lived, and that he would try to contact him as well.

As soon as we left the clinic, Ahmed was yammering to get a

hired car. We dropped him off, and then Neila, and went back to our hotel. I telephoned the Embassy to tell them that the brother had set out, but very strange things happened during the call. Literally every few seconds the line went dead; somewhere down the line someone was pulling the plug on our call. The diplomat finally managed to get put through to my room, and just had time to say, "I don't think this phone is safe any more," before we were cut off. He called again to say, "You may be under surveill . . ." then the line went dead.

If we were under surveillance, I cannot think why we were not picked up. Ben and I sat nervously in my room for a couple of hours. We tried to contact our London office, but kept getting cut off again. We thought we were on the point of arrest and debated whether we should get to the Embassy at once. But that would mean missing the girls if they came out that night. We bit our nails. We tried to think what we would say if we were arrested. We suspected they would accuse us of spying, and if they did, we were in trouble. We hoped they would just deport us — at least then we would have the story — but Ben was terrified they would destroy his film. We paid a very brief visit to Neila's house and left the film, the notebooks and tape-recording there, in a box hidden under one of the floor mattresses.

To try and kill time, and because we felt safer in a crowd, we walked round the market. Ben bought a pot, a great big ugly thing. He said it might come in handy, and it was the sort of object tourists would buy. We walked until seven in the evening, then returned to the hotel. There was a call from the Embassy to say that beds in a "safe house" had been arranged for that night. The couple whose home was to be used would be waiting for us all to arrive. The call was again interrupted by the line going dead every few seconds. He repeatedly phoned to tell us that it was essential, if the children were to be entered on their mothers' British passports, that they have their birth certificates. I told them the girls had none, but that I had got the birth dates. He said that they would have to get a priest or lawyer who would make an affidavit that the children belonged to their mothers. I called Neila and she said that would be no problem. They had a family friend who was a lawyer and he would come to the house that night. Everything was set. All we had to do was wait.

We had arranged with the family in Taiz that we would wait to hear from them. When they rang, it would be to say that Ahmed was back. The minutes dragged by. At nine o'clock, Neila rang: "Ahmed is back — alone," she said. Ben and I hopped into a taxi and were at the house ten minutes later.

Ahmed was again sitting wretchedly on the floor. He had gone to the villages, but the men would not let him see his sisters. They suspected he was planning to take them away. Furthermore, they had informed the police who had come that day that Ahmed was a troublemaker and a thief. Several things had gone missing from the village during the time he had stayed, they said. If he ever came back, the villagers would have him arrested. He had not even glimpsed his sisters; they would think we had all abandoned them.

We were all bitterly disappointed. I alerted the Embassy and told them what had happened. They agreed that the best thing that Ben and I could do was to get to Sana'a quickly in the morning. They told us to catch a plane from Taiz airport, and that the Consul, James Halley, would meet us.

We told the family about our interrupted phone calls, and Neila said: "It is quite probable that you are being followed now. We want to help, but Mum is not all that well, and it would be better if you didn't come any more, at least not during the evening. We have been watched before and it could happen again."

She said it was only a pity that the villagers were now so suspicious. "If only they had gone with Ahmed the week before when he brought his car, then they could have slipped away without anyone noticing," she said. "The stuff about them getting exit visas from Yemen could have been sorted out. Officially, wives travelling outside Yemen are meant to get their husbands' permission, but no one does. Mum, for example, is always coming over to England, and she never gets Dad's permission. There is a visa office in Taiz and you just go in and get it stamped. It is much easier here than in Sana'a. We could have sorted that out for the girls, but now the visa office has probably been alerted by the villagers."

It had also been alerted by the police chief, but we were not to know that. Neila was anxious. She repeatedly went to the window and peered out into the street. "I've got a feeling that you should go now," she said to us. We agreed — the last thing we wanted to do was jeopardise the family who had helped us so much. We promised Ahmed that things would happen; that we were going straight to the Embassy the next day to tell them about the sisters and to demand action. We would only make one more visit to the family's home — to collect what we had left in the box.

That night I hardly slept, thinking every noise in the hotel was a squad of the National Security Police. When I finally did doze off in the early hours, it was only to be woken at dawn by the Imam singing his call to prayer. At eight o'clock in the morning, I telephoned Jim Halley, the Consul. He told me the flight times, and we agreed on the one o'clock flight. He promised that he would be waiting at the airport in Sana'a to meet us.

We made a lightning visit to Neila's home to collect our precious belongings, then caught a taxi, first to Yemenia Airways ticket office. By this time we were as jumpy as cats on a hot tin roof, but everything went smoothly. Rather than return to the hotel we got to Taiz airport three hours early. In an upstairs waiting-room, crammed with soldiers who all appeared to be going on leave to Sana'a, I started to write up the interview with the girls. In case we were arrested, I wrote it as a diary, with lots of mentions of camels and "nice view".

The jet was on time. As we passed through armed guards to get to the tarmac, Ben was stopped, although I was allowed to go on. I hung around waiting, wondering whether I should continue if he was detained. But they were only interested in his cameras and once he had shown the guards how they came apart, he was waved through.

It was a 25-minute flight, and sitting in first class we were very aware of our scruffy appearance beside wealthy Yemeni businessmen. I still had on my one pair of cotton trousers and a top that Neila had given me. We landed at Sana'a, and as it was an internal flight, we did not have to change money. Our passports were examined and handed back to us. We were hardly breathing by this stage, just anticipating the heavy hand descending on our shoulders.

Then we had to wait for half an hour for our luggage. Sitting on a stationary carousel, looking out at the crowd, I saw a man who I thought was Jim Halley. He looked like a Consul somehow: grey hair and wearing a white shirt and tie. There were other Europeans, but I was certain that was our man. He was staring at us, too. He told us later that we were easy to spot because we were the only two Europeans on the flight, but in our nervousness we had not noticed. Then he raised a hand and gave a little wave. We waved back.

Finally our luggage came off the plane. We merged with a group of women and children, and suddenly we were past the last guards. Jim came over and shook hands. As we walked to the car park, I said: "Why aren't you doing something to help the girls?"

Jim retorted sharply: "Believe me, we would if we could."

Chapter Fourteen

We climbed into the bullet-proof, riot-proof diplomatic jeep. Jim told us that the Ambassador, Mark Marshall, was anxious to meet us, so after we had checked into a hotel he would like to see us immediately. I explained that we were worried about National Security, and Jim said: "Right, we'll go straight to the residence."

He was a friendly, open Scotsman, genuinely concerned about the Muhsen sisters. On our way to the residence, he told us that he, his wife and family had only been in Yemen for six weeks. The Ambassador had arrived three weeks ago, and they had all been suddenly dumped with the Muhsen case. Mr Marshall had not yet presented his credentials to the President of Yemen, and therefore, officially, did not yet have Ambassador status. I asked about Mr Page, the Vice Consul. "He left," said Jim shortly.

We had arrived at the heavy metal gates which marked the official residence of the British Ambassador and his family. Jim tooted, and an armed guard opened a small door in the gates, scrutinised him, then the gates swung open. Just inside the grounds was a guard post with two soldiers. Eight guarded the residence at night, patrolling the grounds. Inside, heavy doors at the foot of the stairs leading to the first floor bedrooms were locked at night, and bars placed across so that if anyone broke in they would have to saw through wood and metal to get to the family.

We swung up the driveway, and the Ambassador's wife, Penny, met us at the door. We went into the drawing-room, and she served us with tea. It all seemed terribly English, and Ben and I felt even more like a couple of hill-billies coated in dust. Mr Marshall came in and introduced himself, and we all sat down nervously. Ben and I were wondering if he was going to be more of a hindrance than a help; he appeared anxious about what I was going to write. He warned me that an article too critical of the Yemeni authorities could have severe consequences not just for the sisters, but for the British community.

I asked why no one from the Embassy had been to see the girls, why it had taken two journalists to find them. He said that his staff could not do what we had done. For a British diplomat to have gone into Mokbana without notifying the authorities would have been disastrous. It would have soured relations, to put it mildly. His staff of ten people could not travel in Yemen without first getting permission from the Government.

Why, then, I asked, were not greater efforts made to send in the Embassy's agent in Taiz, Alan Herbert? This was the man who had asked Neila's family to find out about the sisters.

"It would have jeopardised him to have gone to Mokbana, as it would jeopardise any British person," said Marshall. "I only hope that the people who helped you have been discreet, and will not be in trouble themselves."

He asked us to tell him what we had found. He said: "You are independent witnesses. Everything we have had so far on this case has been through a number of agencies; we have had virtually nothing from the mother."

I said this was probably because of the treatment she received from the Embassy when she visited in April 1986.

"But what we can't understand is why she did not return with the tape to play it to us here — why she went back to England, did nothing for a year and then told the story to the Press," said Jim.

I told him that she had not returned to the Embassy because of Page, but she had sent the tape to Cantwell in Geneva, and since then his charity had been trying to force the Yemenis into taking action. She had only released the story to the Press as a last, desperate act.

We told them how we had found the girls and their story. We explained about family X and all the help they had given us; our various plans with Ahmed. They were curious to meet Ahmed, and I told them they would probably do so quite soon, because he wanted to apply for a British passport. "How many more Muhsens are going to pop up?" they groaned.

Mr Marshall then said that he was very keen for us to meet a representative from the Yemeni Ministry of Foreign Affairs. "I wonder if they have known all along that you were here?" he mused. "I am not normally a great advocate of the conspiracy theory, but in this case, I am not so sure. It is incredible that you have done what you have without being picked up. That is what makes me suspicious that they have been quite aware from the moment you arrived."

Ben and I thought this was extremely unlikely, and with hindsight, I can only think it was inefficiency that prevented National Security catching us. The Ambassador said that we would have to play it very carefully if we did manage a meeting with the Foreign Affairs department. He said: "I would like them to hear it from you, as you have been there and seen everything for yourselves. We would have to say that you were journalists, but visiting Yemen on tourists' visas, which is true. If they wanted to they could get nasty about that, because you have broken the law. They would probably only deport you, but that wouldn't matter."

"It would if they destroyed my films," interjected Ben. We asked if it would be possible to send the films in the diplomatic bag on the next flight, which was the following morning. Marshall said no, he could not agree to that. We decided, after a great deal of discussion, that either Ben would go back himself in the morning, with his film, so that the paper would have it by Friday night, or that he would give it to a British person to take for him. We could not see the Foreign Affairs official until Saturday, because Friday was the Arab Sabbath, and the offices were closed.

Mr Marshall went off to telephone the official, leaving Ben and me to debate. We asked if it was all right to have a walk in the grounds to talk. We still did not know whether to fully trust the Embassy. Mrs Marshall said that the guards might be suspicious of us walking about outside, and if they approached us, we were to call. It would not do if we got shot at this stage.

Outside, we discussed what we should do. I felt it was important to see the official if it could be arranged. Ben was worried about entrusting his film to strangers. He felt he should go personally in the morning. We went back inside and told Jim and Mr Marshall that we had decided I should stay, but that I wanted to ask why the Yemenis, who were aware of the situation through various agencies, for example Defence of Children International, had done nothing. Mr Marshall responded with a twinkle: "Eileen, you must learn that the combative approach is not always the best." He was also apt to say: "With all due respect, Miss MacDonald . . ." in not such a twinkling way.

Throughout the evening he tried various officials at home, but could not track down the right one. He copied Zana's tape and said he wanted to play it to the official when we met him. I was not too keen on being deported, but the Ambassador said that a diplomat would be with me during the meeting. He asked if we had booked in to a hotel yet. We again explained that we were concerned about being picked up by Security, and the Ambassador, after a brief chat with his wife, said: "Oh, I think we have a couple of spare beds for you here."

Ben and I were very relieved. I think if we had had to book into a hotel, we would not have slept a wink. We telephoned the newspaper and were told that they wanted the story for that Sunday's paper, so there was no question of Ben remaining. If I could see the official, and obtain a promise of action from the Yemenis, so much the better for the story. I was to stay. Mr Marshall had told me that it would probably be better for me if I was not in the country when the story appeared; he did not know how the authorities would react. If, of course, we did have a meeting on Saturday, and it had a favourable outcome, then being in the country on Sunday would not matter. It would all depend on the reaction to the story.

The office were keen that I should file the story by Friday night, but worried that the call would be intercepted and I would be cut off. I was told to write the story that night, legibly, and send it with Ben in the morning. That would mean sitting up most of the night.

We were all now much more relaxed with each other. Ben and I were convinced of the Embassy's concern for the sisters, and the formal overtone of the first half of the meeting had gone. We were offered a meal and only then realised that we had not eaten all day. It was served to us in the stately dining-room by the butler-cum-housekeeper.

Afterwards, I telephoned Neila to see if there was any news.

Zana, December 1988.

Marshall warned me that his phones were tapped, so to be careful of what I said. He added that I could not use his phone to file my story the next day, and I suppose if I had done the listeners would have got an earful direct from the Ambassador's residence. Neila told me that Ahmed had gone back to the villages that afternoon in spite of the arrest threat. He had seen his sisters and told them we had gone to the Embassy, and help would come soon.

Back in the sitting-room, Ben was showing Mrs Marshall how to use his camera. We debated how best to conceal the story I was going to give Ben. I had an exercise book in which I could write it, and I had written "My Diary" on the cover. Still, if it was confiscated, or even worse, read and understood, we would all be in difficulties. Then, if, while I was sending the story by phone I got cut off, the paper would be minus the story altogether. We had to ensure the story Ben carried was safe, but how?

Marshall's 12-year-old daughter, Frances, came up with a good idea. "Why not send it on different bits of paper inside Christmas card envelopes?" she suggested. Her mother added: "Every British person on the flight will be carrying Christmas cards. We could send it safely inside those, and they would never open them." Frances ran off to get a supply of cards, but I was worried that there could be a disaster and the cards would be opened. It would look very suspicious to a guard — bits of paper with writing on, concealed away.

We decided a safer idea would be to tear the pages from the exercise book, crumple them up and stuff them in Ben's ugly pot. No self-respecting soldier would give it a second glance, and if they did it would just look like rubbish. "I knew it would come in handy," Ben said smugly.

His flight was at nine in the morning. He was to be picked up by another British diplomat going home on leave at just after six. I would be writing, I thought, all night. One version for the pot, another to read out over the phone — and they both had to be legible.

We were shown to our rooms upstairs. I looked longingly at the bed; all I wanted to do was sleep. I was shown the upstairs sitting-room, next to my room, by Mrs Marshall. She thoughtfully provided me with a kettle and a jar of Nescafé and milk. I wrote until five the next morning, then, too wide awake to sleep, read a thriller I had brought along. Ben came in at 5.30 a.m. and scrunched up my precious words to shove them in his pot. He left, and I slept for a couple of hours.

It was a beautiful day, temperatures soaring into the high eighties. I thought I may as well sleep outside in a chair, but I reckoned without Frances and her older sister, Charlotte, who demanded that I play ping-pong. Eventually in the late morning their parents took them out for lunch, and I went back to bed. I woke up again after four and Mrs Marshall took me on a guided tour of the old city. It was beautiful, tiny streets and high buildings of stone, with little decorated windows. I was only sorry that I was not able to appreciate it all properly — I was still half asleep.

I had arranged to file the story at 7 p.m., which would be 4 p.m. in London. Jim picked me up in his jeep to take me to the telephone exchange where there were international booths. Unfortunately the entire population of Sana'a was queueing at the international phone, and it did not take incoming calls. We decided to go to the Taj Sheba Hotel and ask if I could use a phone there.

On our way we ran into a riot, although the Ambassador later insisted it was only a football-match crowd going home. It did not look like that; men were running and shouting in the street, waving red flags. Jim thought it could have been a protest at the announcement that day that several North Yemenis were to be executed in the southern part of the country for subversive activities.

The lady who called everyone "love" was behind the reception desk. She assured Jim and me that it would be no problem, love, to use the phone at a table in the main foyer. Jim said that he would have to leave me; there were turkeys arriving on a flight from England. A Christmas lunch for expats was being held at the residence on Sunday, and if I was still around, I could help prepare the Brussels sprouts. I thought being part of the family was all very well, but I drew the line at the thought of cleaning a ton of Brussels sprouts.

I was connected easily to the office, and filed the story. I thought as I was loudly and slowly enunciating the words to the copy-taker that the entire hotel could be listening in to the exclusive story. I wondered if the *Sunday Mirror* had just arrived and were sitting behind a pillar, gratefully writing down the report verbatim. After I had finished, I went back on to the newsdesk to say I would be around for another hour at the phone if there were any queries. Then I took out my thriller and became immersed in it.

I looked up when I heard a cough. A very well-groomed Yemeni man was standing over me, in Western clothes. He smiled and snatched the book at the same time: "What are you reading?" he asked. It was a book about how some Jewish terrorists hi-jacked a plane.

I said: "Just a thriller."

He looked at it carefully, but as he was holding it upside down, I doubt whether he understood it. He held on to it, still smiling. "A week ago I was on the same flight as you and your husband," he said. "Then you came here, and I was here too. I am the Sales Director of the Taj Sheba. Then you went to Taiz. I know because I was in Taiz too. Yesterday you came back to Sana'a. I know because I was on the same flight as you."

What a coincidence, I thought, wishing Jim were here and damning the turkeys. I smiled back at the man and said brightly: "Isn't Yemen a beautiful country?"

"Where is your husband?" he asked, the smile sticking to his face.

"Er, he has gone home to visit his sick mother," I said.

"Where have you been staying since you came back to Sana'a?" he demanded, the smile slipping.

"With some friends of ours," I said.

"Which friends? What do they do? Where do they live?" came the staccato questions.

"Engineering friends," I said.

Suddenly he grabbed my sheets of paper with the story written on. This time he got them the right way up. It was page one, headed "I go to Sana'a — my diary". He only had to read past that to discover it was a very curious diary about how two British girls had been tricked into marriage and were living as virtual prisoners in Yemen. He flicked through the sheets. "You are doing research. Why?" he said.

I had no lingering doubts that he was a Sales Director; I

wondered whether they tortured people before they deported them. Jim would not be coming back until I telephoned him at home to say I was ready. His house was ten minutes away.

"It's just a diary," I said, reaching up and snatching it back. "Yemen is so beautiful that I do not want to forget a minute."

"When you arrived you looked like someone from England. Now you have a suntan and wear our head-dress," he said. "I go to England a lot and it always rains." Suddenly he stood up straight, shook hands and said: "If there is anything I can do to help you, I am in that office there," and he pointed to a small room beside the reception desk. He left me then, wondering if in fact he was who he said he was after all.

The office phoned through and said the copy was fine. They also told me that Ben's flight had been badly delayed and he was not expected in London until the early hours of Saturday. I told them a little of what had just happened, and they insisted I leave the country the next day, or else they would hold back the story. My next call was to Jim. I told him a little of my meeting and he arrived at the speed of light.

On our way back, he told me that he was sure there was no Sales Director at the Taj Sheba. He knew the staff well, and he had never met the man I described. "What I can't understand is why he did not arrest you," said Jim. "Maybe he had gone off to use the telephone in his office to call in the troops."

The Ambassador was equally curious about my interrogator. I relayed the news that the London office were anxious for me to depart quickly and he agreed. "I think we should just try tomorrow to get you in to see the Minister, though," he said.

That night I helped unpack Christmas lunch supplies, under the curious gaze of the soldiers on guard duty. In the morning, at 7.30 a.m., I was up waiting for the Ambassador to get through to the Ministry. It took all day before the right person was found. I was up dozing in the sun on the flat roof when the Ambassador came over. "They say that I can phone again tomorrow to try to arrange a meeting. I impressed upon them that the important person was leaving tonight, but it made no difference. I will tell them what you have told me and play them the tape." We had to leave it at that.

I ventured out on my own about 200 yards down the road to

buy a ticket at Yemenia Airways for the 1 a.m. flight to Rome. I
could get a flight from there to London the next day, but the
important thing was to be out of Yemen when *The Observer*'s story
broke late on Saturday night.

The Ambassador walked me round to the Taj Sheba to get a
taxi to the airport. The BMWs gleamed in the darkness, and a
young man detached himself from the pack of drivers to approach
us. It was Sultan. "Mrs Ben," he cried. "Where is Mr Ben?" I told
Sultan Mr Ben had gone back home because he was unwell, and
now I was following him. I told the Ambassador that this was our
long-lost driver, Sultan, and I thought he was trustworthy. I
thanked him and his wife for putting up with two journalists at
such short notice, but said I was relieved to be missing out on the
Brussels sprouts.

Sultan, clearly delighted to have found "Mrs Ben", was
standing, holding open the door. Gratefully, I climbed into the
familiar back-seat, and we purred away. Even then, I was
wondering whether he might turn round, waving a Luger, and
drive me to the nearest torture chamber. But he only made a last
bid for my address. I was tempted to give him Ben's, but resisted.

The flight was delayed for two hours, and I thought that was
bad enough. When I eventually arrived back at the London
office, Ben told me his was delayed for 12 hours, and he had
resorted to weeping in front of the airport manager to get on a
flight.

Just before 3 a.m. the sound of an approaching aircraft jerked
me awake. I had been dozing, having a vivid nightmare about
being shot in the neck. Dopily, everyone in the waiting lounge
queued up, and half an hour later I was looking down at the lights
of Sana'a. Now, as one of the most *persona non grata* people on
Yemen's hate-list, I doubt whether I shall ever see them again.

Chapter Fifteen

When I walked through the Arrivals Hall at Heathrow Airport, Paul, my fiancé, was waiting, waving a copy of that morning's *Observer* in his hand. The story, with Ben's picture of Nadia holding Tina in her arms, was on the front page. It was a great relief. I had feared it might have ended up on the foreign page.

We went back to our new home — in the time I had been away, we had moved house. I had been in for about an hour and we were demolishing a bottle of champagne, when the telephone rang. It was the BBC Radio Four programme, *Today*. Would I come in that evening to be interviewed for Monday's show? I was surprised; I did not think the story would have appealed to *Today*, but I agreed.

I telephoned Miriam. She was emotional, but delighted with the story. We talked briefly and I said I would be coming up to Birmingham on Tuesday to tell her everything. I said that there had been a change of staff at the Embassy; they were now very keen to help. "Nadia looks much worse in the picture now than when I was there," she said.

I did the radio interview at the *Today* studio, then went to sleep. The next morning at 10.30, the telephone rang. BBC Television *World at One* wanted to interview me immediately in time for their show. I put the phone down, and it rang again; Central Television wanted an interview. Then it was ITN, *The Six O'Clock News* and *News At Ten*. By the end of the day, I had lost count of the number of interviews. I was rather dazed at the intense interest. The story had taken off in a big way. Then the other national papers began phoning my home, asking for follow-ups, telephone numbers. I was asked if *The Observer* had "bought" Miriam — paid her money so that her story was exclusively ours. We had not.

American news companies phoned, Italian television too; it was their lead item. In the course of the week the story was syndicated world-wide. I had letters from Australia, Kuwait, Hong Kong.

On Monday night, I watched the news. ITN carried the story, interviewed Miriam, then me, then instead of Muthana Muhsen saying he had done nothing wrong, as he had been doing all day, there was an interview with the Yemeni Ambassador, Mr Ahmed Alazeib. He produced a tape-recording — Zana's first tape — saying that she was happy and talking about killing a goat for Christmas. It was 21 December. Although the tape was seven years old and Zana sounded like a robot, it seemed to be contemporary. The Ambassador had been sent the tape by Muthana and was playing it to rebut our story. It was all lies, according to the Ambassador. Watching the interview, I was seething, but there was little I could do.

On Tuesday morning I went to work. My first task was to locate Miriam so that Ben and I could visit her to tell her all the news that had not been published. She was not at home. I telephoned Mr Marshall, and he told me that the Ministry of Foreign Affairs had seen the story. On Monday morning they had informed him that they were prepared to meet him the following day, which was today, and that he had just come from that meeting. They had listened attentively to the story I had told him. They also listened to the tape, and had it translated. "It was a very fruitful meeting," he told me. There had been a certain amount of anger — and amazement — that two journalists had got not only into Yemen, but Mokbana, on tourist visas. "There was a certain amount of seething going on," he said.

It was so fruitful that later in the morning the commander of Mokbana drove into the girls' villages in a jeep. He had with him his squad of police officers. His men had been in the previous week looking for us, but this was a different mission. They had come for Zana and Nadia. The girls knew nothing until they were called by village women to get ready quickly, an important man had arrived. There was a brief meeting, during which Zana told him their story. The commander told the girls he was taking them to Taiz. The Government had recalled their husbands from their work in Saudi Arabia. Zana told me later: "He said we would go to meet our husbands, but he would be there. Lots of important

Nadia, Ahmed, Tina, a cousin and Haney, February 1988.

people wanted to talk to us. He was very kind. He wanted to know if we had known you were journalists. He said it was not the best way to have got help, but he understood.

"He told us to get ready, and bring our things. I did everything in about two minutes, so did Nadia. We had the kids dressed and were holding them. Then the commander said: 'No, not the children. They stay here, you can collect them later.' We said, 'No, we must bring the babies.' There was no one to look after them except Gohad's mother, who was 91 and blind. He was very gentle with us, but he said we first of all had to publicly accept our husbands. If we did, we could come back and collect our children; he swore there would be no problem. We both said immediately: 'We accept them, then,' but he said we had to write a letter in Taiz before our children could be with us. It was blackmail, but we couldn't do anything else."

The girls got into the jeep, and their journey out of Mokbana began. "I didn't believe what was happening," said Zana. "I kept thinking either I'd wake up, or someone would stop us." On their arrival at Taiz, the commander took them first to his home. There, looking extremely uncomfortable, were their husbands, one grossly overweight, Nadia's husband, Mohammed. The other, tall and skinny, was Abdullah. The sisters had not seen them for two years, but there was no joyous reunion. The men were scared and trembling; they thought they were in serious trouble, having been notified by the Governor of Taiz at their homes in Saudi Arabia, to get to Taiz in 24 hours. "They couldn't wait to get to the telephone to tell their fathers," said Zana. "They were terrified at what was going to happen to them, and they had to get instructions."

The first call the men made was to Gohad, in Birmingham, who was dismayed to hear that action had been taken. He had already been in touch with Abdullah's father in Saudi Arabia, and both men had talked at length to Muthana, to work out what was the best course of action. "Do not divorce; don't let the girls have the children," the sons were told. "They will never leave their kids, so they will never come home. We don't want them here." Abdullah's father told him: "Do this for me; it will bring great shame on me if you come here with Nadia; she will talk even more about what happened."

As soon as the calls were over, the girls had to write a letter, addressed "To whom it may concern", that they publicly accepted that they were married to their husbands, and happy with them. The commander ordered them to copy a letter he had written: that they were now living in Taiz and their problems were over. "You will get your children back at the end of the week," he told them when they had finished.

He promised the girls that if they decided to stay in Yemen, they would live in Taiz, in a fine house which he would provide. He offered the family a new life, one in which they would never again have to live in Mokbana. He would provide the men with work, and the girls could see British women who were happily married in the town. The girls stuck to their guns. "We want to go home," they chorused. Their husbands, after more telephone calls for permission, said they wanted to stay in Taiz, but with their wives and children. The commander said that the sisters must not be held against their will, and if the husbands could get themselves into Britain, with their wives, they would all be home in ten days. "We did not really believe him," said Zana. "He was crafty, and we knew he took bribes. But we could not really say anything. We still thought we must be dreaming, anyway."

The meeting drew to a close, with the couples glowering at each other, deeply mistrustful. The commander, Abdul Walli, decided to let them all think it over for a few days. The unhappy foursome were taken to a flat, near his house. They were to live there for a week, they were told, then get their children back, then go home to Britain. The girls were dazed that after seven years, their ordeal seemed to be careering to an end. "We had to sleep with our husbands again, but they were so scared, they didn't touch us," said Zana. The next day, one of the commander's men appeared at the flat, and took them to the commander's house. The girls were led into an office and were told they could telephone their mother.

Shaking, Zana dialled her home in Sparkbrook. Her sister, Aisha, answered. "She didn't believe it was me. She asked me all sorts of questions, like who I had fancied at the youth club, before she would accept it. She was crying, she kept saying: 'It can't be you, Zana.'"

Zana asked for her mother, but Aisha said: "We haven't seen

her. Alf Dickens has taken her away somewhere. We don't know where she is."

Back at *The Observer* office I was having exactly the same difficulty. Miriam had vanished, and no one knew where she was. If I had only but known it, Miriam was less than a mile away, sitting in the offices of the *Daily Mail*.

I telephoned Alf Dickens' number. His wife answered. She sounded very confused. She said: "I don't know where Alf is either. He said yesterday that Miriam was going to crack up with all the television interviews and the reporters, so he has taken her away to rest. He wouldn't tell me where they were going, but he promised to telephone me tonight." I left a message, asking that Miriam should contact me.

Then Fleet Street rumours began. Various papers were climbing over each other to offer Miriam money for the exclusive story. She had been bought, I was told, although by whom, I did not know. *The Sunday Times*, *The Observer*'s direct rivals phoned me. Incredibly, a reporter asked me to give him all my contacts in North Yemen, because he wanted to go and find the girls too. I replied with something along the lines of "You must be joking." Then there was a call from the *News of the World*. They wanted to send a woman reporter to Yemen, they said. Could I tell them how to go about it? Another joker. The Embassy of the Yemen Arab Republic, that week, suddenly had a flood of visa applications for holidays to Yemen. Everyone was refused, even valid holidaymakers.

I was anxious to find out what had happened to Neila and her family; we had promised to keep in touch. When I telephoned her number, she answered, but as soon as I said who I was, she said in a very frightened voice: "I'm sorry; I cannot take this call. Goodbye." I immediately telephoned the British Embassy to find out if they knew if anything had happened to the family. They had not heard, but promised to investigate. A month later, when Neila returned to Britain, she told me that just after *The Observer* ran the story, she was picked up and taken to National Security Police headquarters. She was interrogated for several hours, then told to go home and write a statement, which she had to hand in at the police station. The Director of the clinic, and Mohammed, our driver, were also interrogated and asked to write statements.

Back home, Neila was quite cheerful about her experience. "They wanted to know if we had known you were journalists at the time. Of course we didn't know. Would we have risked our lives if we had known it was for journalists?" she asked. She was worried, however, that in future she might be refused a visa to travel to Yemen to see her mother and family there. She also told me that a British Red Cross doctor, who had been due to leave Taiz, had not been given an exit visa. This tied in with other information I had received about medics being refused entry visas to Yemen. It seemed that the authorities had decided no British person should be allowed in, in case they turned out to be journalists.

On the same day, Wednesday, 23 December, the Yemeni Ambassador issued a statement. In it he said that he understood the sisters had met and married their husbands in Birmingham seven years ago and had then gone to live in Yemen. Problems had only arisen when Mrs Ali split up from her husband, Muthana Muhsen.

Thus far, it was an amazing statement. Muhsen had already publicly admitted and been reported as saying that he had duped his daughters into marriage, and sent them on a holiday as brides. Furthermore, he had never been married to Miriam.

It became clear that Muhsen had been frantically working on a story that would put him in a better light. It was also reported that he had been seen with the Ambassador in Birmingham the previous week. Whether the Ambassador agreed with him or not, it was a better story and less damaging to Yemen than Muhsen's previous statements.

The Ambassador's statement continued that if, however, "Mrs Ali" wished to visit Yemen, and "sort out the family problems", she would be given every assistance by the Yemeni Government to bring her daughters home.

Zana, in her call home, had left a telephone number in Taiz with her sister. Aisha passed it on to her mother, when she phoned from the *Daily Mail*. On Christmas Eve, Miriam got through to her daughters at the home of the commander. She said: "Nadia would not speak on the phone to me; she is so withdrawn now. As soon as I spoke to Zana, I knew something was wrong. She could not talk much because an official was with her. She said she was worried because the official had told her he was going to get visa application forms for the husbands to come back to Britain.

"She thought that the British Government would not grant them the visas, and that would mean neither she nor Nadia could come home. She kept asking when I was going to come over to be with them. I had to explain that I had to get a visa first."

The previous day Miriam, Alf Dickens, still claiming she would dissolve without him, and two *Daily Mail* journalists had submitted their visa applications to the Embassy of the Yemen Arab Republic. They had put them in together, and were swiftly informed they would not be granted. In the interim, the *Daily Mail* took Miriam and Mr Dickens to be vaccinated for Yemen, so it could be all systems go when the visas came through.

When the rejection for the journalists and Mr Dickens arrived, the *Daily Mail* produced a contract for Miriam, binding her to give them exclusive rights on the story. Miriam said: "They took me into an office, and said, 'Look, we can't come with you, but you can do it all yourself. We will show you how to use a camera, and a tape recorder, and we will still give you £3,500.' They told me to sign the contract and said I would get the money regardless.

"I suddenly realised what they were up to. They were not interested in my kids, they didn't care if they came home. They wanted me to go there and get them their story, even if it meant jeopardising everything. I knew what the Yemenis would do if I went in there recording everything. They would chuck me out, and move the girls so I would never see them again.

"I got up and said, 'No, I'm going home. I won't sign any contract, I'll do it on my own.' I had no idea how I was going to get the money myself, but I did not want any of theirs."

On the night of Christmas Eve Miriam walked out of the *Daily Mail* offices and went home.

Ben and I, of course, knew nothing about this. We had now learned that Miriam was in the clutches of the *Daily Mail*, and doubted whether we would hear from her again. I decided to write a story for the coming Sunday's paper based on the information I was receiving from the Embassy. Ben decided to go to Birmingham to photograph Miriam's other children waiting for news.

Shortly before midnight, Ben called me from Birmingham. As he had been about to photograph the children, Miriam had walked in the front door. Ben was calling me from Anne Sufi's house. Between them, they had managed to calm Miriam down, but she was extremely upset and desperate to go to Yemen to be with her daughters. Ben felt that if we left Miriam alone, Mr Dickens would get hold of her again, and persuade her to sell the story to another newspaper. We agreed that Ben would bring her down to London with him early the next day, and she could stay with me.

It was now Christmas Day. Miriam arrived in the early afternoon with Ben and joined Paul and me, my parents and a friend for lunch. It was not the happiest meal. Miriam was still very upset, but I had managed to contact *The Observer* and they had given the go-ahead for us to pay for her flight and expenses.

There was a sticky moment over the crackers. Our friend, Colin, was discussing the price of Harrods hampers. He had seen one for £1,300 and asked: "What can you get for that money in a hamper?"

Miriam quietly left the table. My mother nudged Colin and said: "A Yemeni bride."

In the evening Miriam tried to get through by telephone to her daughters, but was told by the commander that both girls had gone back to their villages. This was not true. The girls were being kept away from the phone by the Yemeni authorities who had realised that every time they spoke to their mother, the conversation was reported in the British press.

The girls had been allowed, however, to speak to their father who phoned them on Christmas Day. Zana told me later: "He was on the phone for over an hour. He was begging us not to come home, because he said he would die of shame. He kept saying: 'If you love me, don't come home.' Well, we don't love him, he must know that. He said that if we came home there would be a lot of reporters and he would die of shame. He begged us to stay in Taiz until the press had forgotten about the story. I told him he would be lucky. He said he would kill himself if we came home and I said: 'Good.'"

On Boxing Day, Miriam tried the number again, and this time spoke to Zana. It was the first time that her daughter told her that the children were not with them, but being looked after in Ashube by Nadia's elderly relation. Miriam was distraught, but Zana reassured her. "I said it was the only way we could get to Taiz and the children were being picked up the following day because we had publicly accepted our husbands." Again Zana begged her mother to come to Taiz so that she was with them until they were allowed to leave. "We are frightened on our own, Mum," she said. "We need you."

I enquired at the Yemeni Embassy concerning applications for a visa for Miriam. I said I was a friend of hers, and she was very keen to travel immediately to Yemen. I was told that Miriam should come to the Embassy when they re-opened on Tuesday morning; her other application had not been dealt with because she had submitted it with *Daily Mail* journalists.

I passed on to the Foreign Office the telephone number at which the girls could be reached. They were very surprised, but grateful. They obviously had not realised that quite a few newspapers in Fleet Street knew it, and had been trying to talk to the sisters, with varying degrees of success. I spoke to Jim and he assured me, and Miriam, whom he spoke to for the first time on Boxing Day, that he would make arrangements to interview the husbands if everyone was serious about them attempting to come to Britain with the girls.

We talked about why the Yemeni authorities were so keen for the husbands to come home with the girls. Both Zana and Nadia had told me they did not want their husbands; in fact they hated them. Jim told me how upset the authorities had been about the British press coverage. "It was not your story so much they objected to, but the following ones in papers like the *Star*, and others saying all Yemenis should be thrown out of Britain. If the husbands come back home with the girls then everyone will assume the girls are happy enough with them. Of course it is blackmail, the girls will only agree to the visa applications going in because they want their children."

The day after Boxing Day, Miriam returned to Birmingham , where she was hounded by the *Daily Mail*. "They came after me in the street, saying they wanted to pay for the air-fare," she recalled. "I ignored them." Also, on that day, the Yemeni authorities must have decided that the sisters had behaved

Commander Abdul Walli

sufficiently well in regards to their husbands, for their children were collected by jeep from Mokbana and reunited with their mothers.

On Tuesday morning of the following week, Miriam, with her friend, Anne Sufi, came back to London to get her visa. Ben and I met her and we piled into a taxi to take us to the Embassy. When we reached South Street, however, we saw that the Embassy was under a state of siege. Film crews, photographers and reporters were spilling out into the road. Miriam flattened herself on the floor of the taxi, crying, "Don't let them see me", and we drove past. We decided to go to a pub just around the corner, and telephone the Embassy. Ben called as "Mr John Harris", a friend of Miss Ali. He said that Miss Ali was about to call in at the Embassy, but had been frightened at the crowd of waiting media. The gentleman to whom Ben spoke sounded equally frightened, and leapt at Ben's suggestion that it might be easier if Embassy officials came to Miriam. "Where is she?" asked the Embassy official, and when Ben gave him the address of the pub, he obviously quailed. "A pub?" said the good Muslim. "Oh, all right."

Ben and I, thinking that possibly the photographs we had had to attach to our visa forms might now be being used for dartboard practice at the Yemeni Embassy, hid ourselves away in the corner of the pub. At ten minutes to three, two Yemeni men came in, and made a bee-line for Miriam. One of them was carrying a rolled-up newspaper. From inside this, he took an application form, which Miriam completed. She handed over her passport, air ticket, dollars and photographs. The men said they would meet her in the street outside in 20 minutes, but that she was not to approach the Embassy because of the Press.

Chapter Sixteen

Miriam stayed with us for two more days until we sorted out flights and return tickets for her daughters and their children. In that time she opened up about her life and the tremendous fight she had had for seven years to bring back her daughters. She fervently hoped she would only be in Yemen a week at the most and then they could return as a family. She had never seen two of her grandchildren, and the day before she left she bought presents for them all. When Ben arrived with the tickets that night, and she saw all their names listed, her face lit up for the first time in a huge smile.

She had arranged that her other children would stay with various family friends; she was frightened at the thought that Muhsen might "get to them". He had appeared on local TV saying that he was going to marry off Aisha and Tina to Yemeni boys; a foolish threat as the only way would have been to drug and kidnap them. Her youngest child, Mohammed, 15, was to stay with Muriel Wellington; her other two daughters with friends.

After her experience of the media circus and the *Daily Mail* in particular she was most anxious to leave Britain quietly. We arranged for her to be "VIP'd" through from Gatwick to Sana'a, which would effectively mean that a member of the Lufthansa flight crew would be with her at all times. I wondered how she would fare on her own; she had told me she was agoraphobic, lived on her tranquillisers and during the time she stayed with us had had virtually no sleep.

We arranged with Jim, during lengthy telephone calls, that he would meet her at the airport, let her sleep after the long flight for a day, and then take her to his home until she received permission to travel to Taiz to be reunited with her daughters. She still remembered her treatment at the hands of Mr Page, and was fearful of another similarly unpleasant Consul.

Jim, however, had talked to her on the phone before she left Britain on New Year's Eve and she reluctantly admitted he sounded friendly enough. But when Ben and I saw her off on the flight, she was still saying: "He will be all right, won't he?"

The authorities in Yemen were alerted to her arrival and she was whisked through immigration and customs. Jim took her to a small hotel, very near his home, which he hoped would confound journalists trying to telephone her at larger establishments. He and his wife, Patricia, were inundated on New Year's Day by the British press demanding an interview with Miriam, but adroitly fended them off. "What a Hogmanay," groaned Jim.

He spent the next day, a Saturday, trying to arrange a meeting with the Ministry of Foreign Affairs, who had insisted on seeing Miriam before she travelled to Taiz. His attempts were unsuccessful; everyone was too busy to see them. At about ten o'clock in the morning, after three frustrating hours, Jim decided to take Miriam to the offices anyway. He reasoned that they were unlikely to turn away the woman whom they had promised to assist in every way, if she actually appeared on their doorstep.

He left Miriam in the diplomatic jeep. Three and a half hours later, he came out of the building, seething. He told Miriam: "They say, 'No go' today, and have told us to come back on Monday. I'd like to know what they are playing at." Jim also informed Miriam that the officials he had seen had asked her not to telephone the girls until they had met her and explained their position. They were both very angry, but agreed it was best at this stage to play the game the Yemeni way.

Their patience was rewarded the following day. Jim had gone to the Ministry on different business, and for the first time met some "very friendly officials who were in a good mood, and asked if there was anything else they could do to help the British Consul".

Jim immediately leapt in: "I happen to have a rather distraught mother at my house, helping my wife prepare the Sunday lunch," he said. "Any chance of getting a meeting arranged for her today?" The official said he would see what he could do, and Jim went home.

At 6 p.m., Jim got a telephone call. He was to return to the Ministry offices immediately. He was back home an hour later to tell Miriam the good news, that they were booked on to a flight the following morning. He said the Sana'a officials had been most helpful, and wished her every success in her attempts to resolve the family problems.

Sana'a airport lay swathed in fog the next morning. Miriam, who had forgotten her sleeping tablets and had spent a sleepless night, bit her nails and waited. Jim was scarcely less impatient and at screaming point by the time they made their third trip to the airport only to be turned back because of the fog. Finally, in the afternoon, it lifted, and the Dash Seven jet took off. Travelling with Miriam and Jim was an official from the Ministry in Sana'a and a Yemeni employed as a translator for the Embassy. "My Arabic is pretty good," said Jim, "but it is not perfect. I wanted someone on our side to tell me what the whispered asides meant."

On their arrival at Taiz, Miriam found she was booked in at the Mareb Hotel; Jim had a room at a less prestigious establishment, which, however, according to him, served much better food.

Miriam had been in her room for less than an hour when reception called: the commander was waiting for her. He had asked Jim whether he wished to accompany Miriam to the reunion, but he had no desire to play gooseberry to Miriam and her daughters.

Ten minutes later, Miriam was shown into the commander's home. There she embraced her daughters and tried to hug her grandchildren, but they screamed in fright at the strange white woman. It was 21 months since Miriam had seen the girls. They spent 12 hours alone together, Miriam opting to stay overnight with her girls at their flat. She found Nadia "like a rape victim, with that look in her eyes". Zana, always the strong, big sister, dissolved at the sight of her mother. "We just cried," Miriam said simply.

Early the next morning, Jim arrived to tell them that there was to be an important meeting in about an hour's time at the office of Al-Usifi, the Governor. Both husbands, who had stayed away from Miriam, were to be present.

He recalled that he found the girls in a "much more cheerful frame of mind". He added: "Zana was quite impish; Nadia not as withdrawn as I had expected. Obviously life in Taiz and being with their mother again had improved their spirits enormously. Nadia really did seem like a Yemeni girl. Time and again when she began to speak it was in Arabic, and she would stop herself, and speak in English."

At the meeting, Jim remembers his first sighting of the husbands. "Two more unprepossessing youths I had not come across," he said. "One was tall and skinny, the other short and chubby. The girls called him Fat-so. Both the husbands looked scared stiff, and very much victims themselves, which in reality they were. In fact, they were the youngest victims, at only 13 and 14 years old, when they were forced to accept their British wives. According to both girls, they had been reluctant bridegrooms and had to be battered into sleeping with them."

At the meeting, Al-Usifi made it clear that if the husbands were granted visas for settlement in Britain, then the girls and their children could leave at once.

Jim had already sent visa application forms to the husbands, but it was claimed by everyone in the room that they had not arrived. He had brought more forms, as a precaution, and said that he would help the husbands to fill them out. First, though, he wanted time alone with the girls to find out if they were genuine about their desire that their husbands accompany them.

"I took them into a small side room and said:'Now look, girls, you have got to tell me the truth. You have said time and again that you were forced into the marriages, and you hate your husbands. Now you want them to go home with you, is that right?' They both said 'Yes', they wanted their kids too and it was the only way. That was good enough for me. They were both of age, and they were British citizens. I was there to carry out their instructions."

For the next couple of hours, Jim, with the help of his translator and the girls themselves, completed the visa applications. Nadia's husband, Mohammed, told Jim that he had amassed £12,000 working in a restaurant in Saudi Arabia for the past seven years. That meant he would pass the Home Office immigration requirement of being able to support himself and his family. His father, Gohad, had lived in Britain for around thirty years, only visiting Mokbana occasionally. If Mohammed had been born after he naturalised, he might be entitled to British citizenship through birth. The other husband, Abdullah, the tall, skinny one, said that he had already been to Britain before as a child for medical treatment. His father, although now in Saudi Arabia, had lived in Birmingham for 12 years, and could also be a British naturalised citizen. Both boys might be eligible for passports if the visa applications were refused.

After hearing this information, Jim felt more hopeful that the husbands might be granted entry to Britain. His chief concern was that, if they were not eligible for British passports, they would be refused visas as husbands of British citizens because of the Home Office "Primary Purpose" rule. The rule states that a visa for a husband or wife will be refused if the Home Office considers that the primary purpose of the marriage was immigration to Britain. There was also the knotty problem that the Home Office officials who would deal with the applications doubtless read the newspapers and watched the news and would know that the sisters had repeatedly told how they had been duped into marriage to men they loathed when they were both under 16. Jim commented: "I thought the boys' chances were now marginal, whereas before, I thought they did not have a hope."

What he did not know was that both husbands had lied on the forms. Abdullah had indeed been to England, but he omitted to tell anyone that he had missed being deported by one day for overstaying his visa. He lied on the form when he said he had never overstayed a temporary length of stay in Britain. The other husband, Mohammed, also lied about his savings. In fact, he did not have a bean.

The truth, however, only emerged several weeks later. For the present, Jim considered the husbands had co-operated, and he had done everything he could to help them come to Britain, with their wives and children. Al-Usifi made one stipulation about the sisters' return home. He considered that the press in Britain followed Miriam's every move, and that to avoid further embarrassment to Yemen, she would have to travel 24 hours in advance of her daughters. "Miriam was not happy with that. In fact, she had to be peeled off the ceiling," said Jim. "She kept insisting that because the marriages were not legal, the Yemenis should let the girls go. Whatever the justice of that argument, the Yemenis considered that the marriages, in Muslim law, were legal. So it was pointless to bang your head against a brick wall with that argument, particularly when both girls were saying what they had been told to say to keep their children — i.e. that they wanted their husbands to come to Britain.

"Zana was very good. She knew exactly what was required of her. She told her mother to calm down, that she did not understand Yemeni ways, and it would be all right to travel separately. Miriam looked a bit taken aback, but after that she stopped screeching and was largely quiet in the meeting."

Before Jim left for Sana'a he took the girls, their children and mother for a drive out of Taiz, halfway up a mountain. Again he asked the girls if they were sure they wanted their husbands in Birmingham; and again he received the same reply. Miriam, however, was a different matter. She kept muttering: "I'm not having those two in my home. I hate them. I'll be pleasant enough until we land in Britain, then I'll wave them goodbye."

When Jim stopped the jeep at a suitably scenic spot, he tried to help Nadia by reaching into the back to pick up her two-year-old daughter. The child screamed in horror, and backed into her mother's legs. "I had never had such an effect on children before," said Jim. "I think the wee girl was just not used to strangers."

The sisters were enchanted to see the sights of Taiz from the mountain. They had a discussion about where Mokbana was, and whether they could see Ashube and Hockail. Zana said later: "You can't imagine what it was like. We had been prisoners all those years, and now we were free. We felt very happy at first when we came out of Mokbana just to be in a town, with people being nice to us. When our mum came, we wanted to block everything else out and just be with her again. When I shut my eyes and thought very hard, we were all back in Birmingham." The girls were in such high spirits that they were playing around, pretending to fall off the ledge they were standing on — to the terror of their mother who hated heights.

Jim left for Sana'a with the forms. Normally, the Home Office take at least six months to respond to a visa application. He hoped

Nadia and Haney, February 1988.

that, with a telegram attached explaining the situation the family were in, the Home Office might consider this a priority case. The forms were sent telegraphically at first to the Foreign Office Consular department, and then forwarded to the Home Office. The officials who were to be dealing with the case were given a background briefing by the Consular department. The Home Office said the applications would go to the top of the pile, and be processed as quickly as possible.

Meanwhile, in Taiz, Miriam and her daughters settled into an uneasy routine. They slept and ate at the flat, then visited the commander's house in the afternoon. There was little for them to do. Miriam found that she was expected to pay for everything; the husbands provided nothing. Finally there was a row and Nadia asked her husband for some of his £12,000. He then told her he had no money.

The husbands bitterly resented Miriam's presence and tried to make her leave by telling Al-Usifi she was a troublemaker. The Governor, at the time, ignored their request. Their resentment probably had a lot to do with the fact that with Miriam in the flat, they were unable to sleep with the girls. Nadia slept with her mother. Zana's obvious hatred for her husband, fuelled by Miriam, made him frightened to make a move. The men sullenly followed the women about, and everyone's nerves became increasingly frayed.

In London, Roy Hattersley issued a statement denouncing the Foreign Office for "making a deal" with the Yemeni Government over the husbands' applications. It read: "The campaign which has now gone on for many weeks has been based on the statement that the two girls were married against their will. I believe that statement to be true.

"In that case the marriages are not genuine either by the standards acceptable to British law or the Muslim religion. As someone who has fought for the admission of many genuine husbands into this country I am not prepared to support an arrangement which shows every sign of being a stratagem arranged by the Foreign Office and the Yemeni Government to sweep the whole matter under the carpet." Hattersley informed the Foreign Secretary, Sir Geoffrey Howe, of his statement, and told him that the Foreign Office should stop doing deals and get the girls home.

Jim was incensed at the statement. He wondered if he could sue Hattersley for defamation. "What does he think I am doing? This isn't a deal; it's what the girls want." He and the Foreign Office were also concerned that such a statement at the current time might enrage the Yemeni Government and they could change their minds without offering every assistance.

However, the statement did not receive much publicity. The Yemeni Government continued with its policy of being helpful while the Home Office made its decision.

At work, I was wading through dozens of letters from readers. Some were extremely sympathetic to the plight of the sisters — people wrote in asking if there was anything they could do to help. One mother wrote: "In 1968 my 13-year-old daughter was sexually assaulted by a local man in a North London park. For 12 years she wore the unbelieving expression of Nadia Muhsen in your paper."

Other letters were from unpleasant racists, most of whom did not sign their names, saying that Yemenis, like all blacks, should be kicked out of Britain and we certainly did not want two more. Some said the marriages had been manufactured simply in order to get the husbands to Britain. Tom Quirke phoned me up to ask if, when I had met the girls, they really did hate their husbands? Was it possible I had been mistaken? A Yemeni man wrote to me saying that Muhsen should be "HANGED, SHOT, STABBED, GIVEN A 999,999 VOLT CHARGE!" A particularly unpleasant letter from a Yemeni gentleman in Leeds read: "Did you know one of the other sisters got pregnant by a black man when she was 14?"

Others wrote to tell me of similar cases — a six-year-old girl who was made a ward of court by her mother in Solihull because she feared that her husband, a Yemeni, was about to take her to his country. The man did, and the child is now believed to be in Mokbana. A 12-year-old girl from Birmingham called Yasmin was also in Mokbana. A Pakistani student wrote, begging me not to use his name, but telling me how young girls at his home in Cardiff were shipped off as brides at the age of 13. "One day they are at school, the next they are gone," he wrote.

I was in touch with Miriam and the girls every second day. Their spirits went up and down, but always they asked: "When will the decision be?" I also was in close touch with the three other Muhsen children in Birmingham. Mohammed told me: "Tell Mum to take care and not to say anything." Wise advice, because Miriam was apt to speak her mind about her hatred of all things Yemeni, particularly men.

On 15 January 1988, Jim came to Britain for a week's leave. On Tuesday, 19 January, he asked me to meet him at the Foreign Office to talk to the News Department. I gave them the latest information I had, which was that two days previously at 6 a.m. on a Sunday morning I had had a phone call from Miriam. She was extremely upset. They had all been in a taxi, going to the commander's house that morning when a man who had befriended them had told them that the husbands would never come to Britain, or allow their children to do so. He also said that the husbands had got themselves jobs in Taiz, and wanted to stay there. Miriam was aware that both boys had received telephone calls and letters from their fathers telling them not to come to Britain. As she knew, in Yemen, no matter what the man's age he always obeys his father. Even if the Home Office granted the men's visas, they would refuse to come to Britain, or allow their children to go. They were very distraught, I told the men from the News Department.

They were sympathetic, but realistic. If the worst came to the worst, the children were very young, and had known no other life than Mokbana. In time, they would forget their mothers.

Shortly after this, a source of mine in the Home Office told me that the decision would be announced by 31 January. The news cheered the women in Taiz only slightly.

Chapter Seventeen

Various stories appeared in the Press about the Muhsen sisters during the long period while they waited for the Home Office decision. The *News of the World* ran one article saying that Nadia was a virtual drug addict, having been fed a drug for seven years by her mother-in-law. The story was totally untrue. Nadia, in fact, in the middle of January, was quite ill; a fever which she had had since the birth of her second child returned.

She told her mother that during the birth a village woman had cut her with a razor blade to speed up delivery. The wound was still open and Miriam was frightened at her daughter's near delirious state. I asked the Embassy if there was a British woman in Taiz who could visit the family and take Nadia to a doctor. But no one was willing to risk gaining the attention of the National Security Police in paying a call on the Muhsen girls.

In the end, a hostel for Yemeni wives with problems took Miriam and her daughters under their wing, and Nadia was accompanied to a clinic. After that life for the women eased a little. They regularly paid calls to the hostel, drank tea with the women and heard their problems. Miriam was told that there were "umpteen" girls in the position of her daughters. The head of the hostel, a very respected Yemeni woman, told her that there were not only British girls sold off into marriage in Yemen, but many Americans. The American Consul was currently engaged in trying to locate several girls. "The American Embassy is very good though," the Yemeni woman told Miriam. "As soon as the mother writes to them, they visit the girls, with new passports. Once they forged bits on the passports and took new photographs of the girls, and changed their names. They took the girls and changed their appearance, then got them out. There are so many unhappy girls here; it is terrible that their fathers have treated them in this way." Even Miriam had to grudgingly admit that not all Yemenis were bad.

The deadline of 31 January came and went; the family were in despair, although the Home Office press desk kept saying : "It won't be much longer." Miriam and the girls believed every rumour they heard: the husbands had been sent money by their fathers to bribe the Governor; they would come to England but not until the summer; they would never come; Muhsen had sent a letter to the Government which would ensure the girls would never leave Yemen; an Arab journalist who phoned them said he could get them out in a week because he knew the President, etc., etc. The women believed them all; their spirits swung from deep depression to high excitement.

One day in the market-place, Miriam and the girls met Zana's brother-in-law, Mohammed Abdul Khada. He told them that they would never be allowed to divorce their husbands and leave Yemen. "Only if Muthana pays back the money he got for the girls, will they be allowed home," said Mohammed.

Miriam commented: "It was more proof of what we knew was true — that he sold them."

Visitors to the flat where they were staying described it as "extremely basic" — just stone floors with cushions or mattresses to sleep on, a Yemeni hole-in-the-floor toilet, and cold water. They also remarked on how Zana did not appear to be very "mother-like" to her son Marcus. The toddler was allowed to clamber out on to the balcony and try to balance along its edge while his mother sat smoking. He was given lit cigarettes to hold, and altogether Zana seemed to lack concern for him.

Miriam noted the lack of love. "Zana would just ignore the baby when he was screaming. Once, I remember, she was washing some clothes and he stood screaming for over an hour beside her. I asked her if she loved him, but she could not answer. Once she kissed him when he was asleep. She said that was when she loved him."

Nadia's daughter, Tina, however, would scream "blue murder" when her mother left a room, and was inconsolable until Nadia returned.

Miriam's son, Ahmed, appeared in Taiz, overjoyed to find his mother and sisters together. Miriam at first thought he was wonderful, then became worried that he might be in league with his father.

Ahmed had received a telephone call from Muhsen telling him that the girls must not come home. In an interview he gave to the Press, Muhsen said that Ahmed hated his mother and would hit her "with a big stick" when she arrived. Ahmed, however, did no such thing. The reunion Miriam had with her son was scarcely less emotional than with her daughters. Through the girls, she told him that she had believed he was happy, that she had no idea of his wretched childhood. Ahmed brushed aside her tears and said he was willing to do anything he could to get his sisters out of Yemen. He was also keen to go to England himself, but said he would wait for his sisters to go first. Miriam helped him send off his application for a British passport to the Embassy in Sana'a. Amazingly, after their involvement in the case, a member of the staff wrote back to Ahmed, asking if he could get a letter from his father, confirming that he was the son of British parents.

Unable to communicate except through her daughters, mother and son still became very close. The only good news he could give her concerning his early life was that Leila had been well looked after and was now happily married in Aden.

Ahmed would disappear for long periods of time, and possibly because of the language barrier and Miriam's hatred of Yemeni men, she began to suspect him of being on Muhsen's side and spying on them. Relations cooled, and Ahmed, confused at his mother's change of heart, miserably trailed them around Taiz. The markets they could have visited, the mosques and historic, beautiful monuments had little attraction for the family. Waiting for the decision, they sat around either at their flat, or at the commander's house. Towards the end, Abdul Walli, whom Miriam had once described as friendly and desperate to help them, also became an enemy. She suspected him of taking bribes, and reporting their every move to the Governor. Much worse, he decided that he would like to marry Zana. He plied Miriam with expensive gifts — including a gold watch. Then he told her that he would be able to get Ahmed out of the army and into Britain. "How can I ever repay you?" asked Miriam. "Do you want money?"

"No," said the commander. "I want Zana as my third wife."

Miriam refused his offer in no uncertain terms and ceased to take her daughters to his flat. The commander, furious at being spurned, began to spread rumours that the sisters would never go home — and that he would personally see to it that they returned to Mokbana. Fortunately, Miriam found a Yemeni family who generously allowed the pitiful women and children to use their home.

The family ate out whenever they could, at one of the hotels or small restaurants. The children clung to their mothers, apparently sensing that they could soon be without them. They were alarmed at the toys their grandmother had brought them; the girls explained they had never seen toy dumper trucks; the little girl had never before seen a doll with golden hair. The children were not used to strangers, and certainly not ones who wore funny clothes and spoke a different language. Their life was the hermit-like existence of Mokbana, where they ran bare-footed on the mountains. Miriam had expected her grandchildren to love her; she was bitterly disappointed at their fear.

For hours on end, they discussed what they would do if the decision was "no" to the husbands' visas. Nadia maintained that she would never leave her children, but that she was also going home. Zana said she was prepared to leave her son; she considered that he was the outcome of rape. If the answer was "yes", that would create its own problems. Neither girl wanted her husband. As each day in which they were forced to be with them passed, their hatred grew; to have to return to Birmingham with them in tow was now unthinkable. The husbands themselves kept saying they did not want to go to Britain. "They were so frightened," Zana recalled. "They thought the British Government would just kick them out again, and they knew as soon as we got home that we would not want them anywhere near us."

To research this book, I visited Birmingham to talk to Miriam's younger children, her friends and, hopefully, Muhsen. It took three days to get Muhsen to talk to me and, when he did, it was difficult to interview him because he kept getting up and running out of the room.

Mrs Sufi, with the help of an Arab journalist who wanted to speak to Muhsen himself, suggested that he might like to come to her house to meet me. He did not want to meet me at all, but as Mrs Sufi had invited me, and he was there, there was little he could do about it. He would not consider running away from me in front of the Arab journalist whom he was desperate to impress as a good Muslim and much maligned man.

For some reason, Muhsen respected Mrs Sufi; she thought because her husband was a prominent member of the Muslim community before his death. With Muhsen in her front room, she telephoned me at the hotel I was staying in. When I arrived Muhsen was sitting talking to the Arab journalist. He turned his head to the wall when I came in. He said: "I remember her. She asked me whether I had sold my daughters." Then he turned to Mrs Sufi and said: "I never done anything wrong. I know I'm clean, honest."

Mrs Sufi and the Arab journalist left us alone. Muhsen had only agreed to come to the house because the Arab journalist was there, and was clearly alarmed when he was left alone with me. He asked immediately: "Are you married?" I said that I was not. "Whore," he said. Then he jumped to his feet and started waving his hands at the street outside. "All these people in this road, they live in sin," he screamed. I pointed out to him that he had never married Miriam who had borne him seven children. That really set him off, jumping up and down and screaming. In between the screams and his running to the door to call the journalist, he said that he had wed Miriam in 1960 under Muslim law and that, if she denied it, it was because she must have forgotten about it. (I asked Miriam if she had a memory lapse over her marriage — her language at the very thought of it convinced me she was telling the truth when she maintained, as she always had, that there had never been any suggestion of marriage to Muhsen.)

Then he started saying that I was a Zionist. That was why I had written the story that had upset the whole Arab world. I was not only a Zionist, but a Zionist whore, to boot. I realised that Muhsen was faintly mad.

In order to calm him down, I asked if he could simply tell me his version of events. "No," he said, peering round the sitting-room door and calling for Mrs Sufi. I asked him a series of questions, to which he replied, "I don't know." The Arab journalist had popped back briefly at this moment and told Muhsen not to be stupid, but to answer the questions.

Left on my own with him once more, Muhsen finally told me his side of the story. It was very difficult to understand him, because he said one thing at the start of the sentence, and another at the end. For example: "The girls did not know about the marriages . . . the girls knew, of course they knew."

However, his version was that he had been worried by the girls' behaviour and preference for black boyfriends in Birmingham. So worried that he decided to marry them off to good Yemeni boys. The final straw had been Nadia appearing in court as a thief. "My name in a court and her a thief," he yelled.

"I arranged the marriages with two good men in Birmingham. Their mother knew about it; she bought them their wedding rings. I showed them photographs of the boys, but they did not know they were going to marry them. I could not sit them down and say to them: 'Look, loves, I am going to send you away to live with your husbands.' They were only 14 and 15, so I told them that they were going to go on a holiday to Yemen. They didn't know."

He broke off with this train of thought then to add: "Of course they knew, I took them to the marriage ceremony."

Then he resumed: "Their mother told the girls on the day before they left for Yemen what sort of things a Yemeni wife is expected to do. But they went on a holiday. When they got there they went into the houses and they said, 'Hello, everybody.' Then the girls started playing around with the boys, but saying, 'Ssh, don't tell your father.' But the fathers said: 'We are not worried because you are married anyway.' The girls were very pleased at what I had done. What a good daddy, they said."

I asked whether there had been any sort of ceremony in the villages. "No," he said. "They got married after one year, they wrote me they were married." He added that he had signed the marriage certificates in Birmingham before the girls went, as a sort of "insurance policy". "In Yemen, men and women are not allowed to touch each other unless they are married. I was worried that if the girls started playing around with the boys, and they got pregnant, then I would be in a lot of trouble. So we did the marriages in advance. But I told the two men, who were their fathers-in-law that if the girls did not like it, they could write to me and I would send for them to come home. As far as I know, the girls are still happy. The men I sent them with are good men, and I trusted them with my daughters to make sure they were happy."

I asked him about the money that had changed hands over his daughters' marriages. He refused to answer any questions on the subject.

He said that he had received "thousands of letters" from his daughters but "because of my circumstances" he could not reply to them. He waxed sentimental: "Nobody loves my daughters better than me; I brought them up; I cared for them. They love me." He threatened that he would "get" Miriam for bringing trouble on him by talking publicly about the girls. "I will make her sorry," he said. He kept insisting that he was a good Muslim, and that it was up to his children that they had chosen to stay with their mother rather than with him. "She is going to pay for it all when she gets back," he said. Then with a few more "Zionist whores" he ran out of the house.

I expected that such a character would have merited the rebuke of the Yemeni community in Birmingham. That was not the case. I talked to the head of the Yemeni School in Birmingham, housed in a rundown church hall. Mr Adnan Saif was a leading Yemeni, he informed me, when I first sat down in his school's office. He had talked to Muhsen and Gohad about what had happened to the girls. He said that he didn't think much of Muhsen as a good Muslim, but thought that he had married his daughters off for their own good.

Saif said that the commander of Mokbana had visited Birmingham in November for medical treatment. He described him as a "good man" and that if the girls had only gone to him to explain how unhappy they were, he would have sorted their problems out. "To go to your newspaper was very wrong," he said.

He then turned to the articles I had written about Yemen. "Why did you not talk about the water pipes in Mokbana?" he demanded. "Why did your pictures make them look as if they were sitting in Ethiopia? Why didn't you take happy pictures of the girls? Why did you pretend to be doctors?" On and on he went, finally saying that Ben and I should have gone to the police with our story, or to National Security, to check our facts.

"They would have deported us. You know that," I said.

"That would not have mattered. You should have told them you are journalists," he replied.

He said that the Yemeni community in Britain did not want the girls to come home. They were worried they would say "more bad things about Yemen" if they did. Bride money was a custom, he said. The father of the bride received money from the husband in case the marriage went wrong.

When I visited Muriel Wellington, who was caring for Miriam's 15-year-old son, Mohammed, the boy told me: "I don't know what the custom is. All I know is that when Mum and I went over there, we saw Mohammed first, that is Abdul Khada's oldest son. He told us that his dad had paid mine £800 for Zana, and £800 for Nadia. When we saw my sisters, they said they had been told £1,300 each. I believe my sisters. Even Abdul Khada's son told us they had been sold."

I tried to speak to Gohad. Mrs Sufi knew where he lived and we drove there at 9.30 p.m. one night. The street was very dark, and at first we got the wrong house. A woman came to the door, and when we asked her where Gohad lived, she was very suspicious. "What do you want to know for?" she demanded. Mrs Sufi said that she was a friend of the girls' mother, and the woman's attitude changed. "Two doors along," she said. "I am sorry; I thought you were reporters. We have had a lot of that sort here." I rang the doorbell at the right house, which was in darkness. Eventually a light went on and there were sounds of a bolt being drawn sharply back. An old man wearing an Arab hat, and dressed in a colourful Arab skirt, peered around the door.

"That's him," whispered Mrs Sufi. I explained who I was, and that I would like to talk to him about his son and Nadia.

"Whose business is it that my son is married?" he said, and shut the door.

I talked to Aisha, Miriam's fourth daughter. She, too, was staying temporarily at Mrs Wellington's. The children were relying on spasmodic telephone calls and very occasional letters from their mother, to tell them any news, and they were also prey to rumour.

Aisha told me that she had been stopped in the street by Yemeni men in Birmingham who had accused her mother of causing trouble by trying to bring her daughters home. They had been told that their sisters would never come back to Birmingham. Mohammed, a quiet boy, and the closest to his mother, had not been to school since his mother had gone to Yemen. "The other kids, they tease me about my sisters, and I am afraid I will attack them," he said. "It is better that I do not go." He was also afraid that his father would hang around his school, and try to talk to him. "I never want to see him again," he said. Mohammed was distressed to hear that both his sisters had said they were prepared to leave their children; his sisters less so. Aisha, who has a three-year-old daughter, said: "I can understand how they must feel. They were forced to go to bed with the men; it is not the same as having a child with someone you love."

In Taiz, the situation was worsening. Zana rowed with her husband over not providing for herself or her child. He walked out, taking his toddler son. He returned within 24 hours with the child, but by that time the women were convinced he had gone for good, with the child. Zana was desperate to leave the country. She telephoned Jim to say that there was now nothing holding her there, because her son had been taken.

To try to ease the situation, Jim suggested that Miriam should fly up to Sana'a for the day, to collect money and her passport, which he had taken to get her visa extended.

Miriam decided to take her daughters and grandchildren too for an awayday. Zana refused to budge, declaring that the Yemenis would never let them fly to Sana'a. She was right. When Miriam, Nadia and her children arrived at the airport, they were turned back. Their photographs were pasted up on a board and the airport guards had been alerted that they were trying to flee the country. They were marched back to the commander's house.

The incident lowered the family's morale even further. Zana said to me that night: "We are prisoners here now. They will never let us leave. Why don't they just put a ball and chain on our legs?"

Chapter Eighteen

I could tell that Miriam would not hold on much longer. It was two weeks after the deadline for a Home Office decision on the husbands' visas had passed and there was still no news. In my phone calls to her, her voice was lifeless; she was frequently in tears. The girls stopped coming to talk on the phone, whereas before they always wanted a brief chat. Zana, in particular, had always delighted in picking up the phone first when I called at prearranged times, to say, "Hello, Alison". Alison Harris was the name I used on the phone in case the call was being tapped. Now she lay in her bed on the floor all day, plagued by a headache that would not go away. The husbands, when they came home from work, were irritable and tense too. Fights broke out, with the men having the upper hand, always threatening to tell the Governor that Miriam would have to be sent home because she was interfering with marital life.

The aborted flight to Sana'a had many repercussions. The authorities in Taiz accused the Embassy of trying to spirit the girls and their mother out of the country. They were further incensed at what they believed was a deliberate "slap in the face" by the British Home Office in delaying giving their decision on the husbands' status. They declared that they would not renew Miriam's visa any longer, and that she would have to go. They were unaware that Jim had already managed to get it extended until early March.

On Friday, 12 February 1988, I called Roy Hattersley's office to see if he was still concerned at the girls' plight. He was very much so, said his assistant, Imtiaz Karim. Hattersley was due to speak to Timothy Renton, the Home Office Minister, the following Tuesday.

On Monday night of 15 February I called a friend of mine who worked for the Home Office. She told me that the decision was "no", and that furthermore it had been made about three weeks previously. "They never stood a chance in hell," she said. "The marriages were not legal." She told me that as far as she was aware the decision would be announced early the next week when the Foreign Secretary, Sir Geoffrey Howe, had "rubber-stamped" it. It was curious that the announcement should depend on rubber-stamping from the Foreign Office, but I was told that in this case, the Home Office had been consulting the Foreign Office at every step of the way on what the decision should be. Sir Geoffrey was in Moscow that week, but would see the documents as soon as he returned.

I was due to call the women the following day, at 4 p.m. their time. I could not give them the decision as definite, but I told them that my information was it was probably going to be "no", and that they would know officially by the end of the week. My source had said the Home Office wanted the family to be told first, by telegram, before the decision was publicly announced.

Miriam took the news surprisingly well. "I'm glad the waiting is over," she said. "I never wanted those boys, anyway, no more than the girls did. But what are we going to do now? Does that mean we are stuck here forever?"

Zana, for once, was with her. She came on the line: "I'll leave my kid, you know that," she said.

I asked if Nadia felt the same way, for I had been told that Nadia's husband was very fond of his children, and did not want to lose them, or his wife. Nadia was fetched from the other room to speak to me. I asked her about her children. "I don't care," she said dully. "If I can take them, I will."

I asked both girls if their husbands would give them permission to leave the country, and they both said, "No."

I called Jim with the unofficial news. He was due to visit the family in Taiz the next day. He said it was now the time for the girls to make the tough decision. They could stay in Taiz with their children. The Governor had promised the husbands jobs — which they were already employed in — and a "big house" for the sisters and their children to live with the men in Taiz. They would not have to go back to Mokbana.

If they insisted they still wanted to leave, they would probably have to file for divorce. The husbands were unlikely to agree, and would contest it. Jim felt that even should there be a court case, it could be speeded up; he knew that the authorities were as anxious to resolve the matter as the Embassy.

Then there was just the possibility that the Yemenis could pressurise the husbands into giving permission for their wives to leave Yemen altogether. In all probability it would be without their children, although on humanitarian grounds, perhaps everyone would appreciate it would not be in the children's best interests to be shipped back to Mokbana and be brought up by a 91-year-old blind great-grandmother.

Later on Tuesday, I called Imtiaz. The conversation between Hattersley and Renton had been cordial. Renton confirmed what I already knew — that the announcement would be made at the end of the week or the following Monday.

On Thursday, I checked with my source again. She had fresh information. The rejection of the visas had been on two counts — one that the girls were domiciled in Britain and under 16 when the marriages were made. Therefore the marriages, under British law, were not legal. The second was that Zana's husband, Abdullah, had been issued with a Deportation Notice in 1986. This referred to his overstaying a temporary visa issued in 1983 when he visited Britain for medical treatment to his heart.

Renton's office had said all hope was not lost. There had been talk that the girls could divorce their husbands, then remarry them, so that the marriages could then be seen to be "legal". The husbands could genuinely reapply for visas on the grounds of being married to British citizens. But, of course, said Renton's office, their applications would be turned down again because it would be obvious they were breaking the Primary Purpose rule. My source and I boggled at such contorted, pointless thinking.

The sisters were to be sent a Home Office telegram which would arrive in the diplomatic bag at 7 a.m. on Saturday 20 February. Jim would collect the telegram and other papers, then catch a flight straightaway for Taiz. He said that the sisters had seemed philosophical about the rejections. "It was something we all knew could happen," he said.

They had not made up their minds what they should do;

whether to immediately ask for divorce, or see what the Yemeni authorities would suggest. They were irritated at the continual presence of Mohammed, Nadia's husband, who followed them everywhere and who, they believed, was spying on them.

Saturday morning dawned. For once the flights were on time and Jim's first stop on arriving in Taiz with his documents was to see the Governor, who held the husbands' passports. The Governor was delighted to see him, and when Jim asked for the passports his face lit up; he thought they were going to be stamped with their entry visas to Britain. Jim told him the news, and his face fell. He put his head in his hands and groaned. He had been hoping that these awkward British women would be out of his hair, but it was not to be.

Jim then showed the contents of the telegram to the sisters and Miriam. It only told them what they had known for five days. A meeting was arranged at 6 p.m. that night, but one of the husbands, Abdullah, was not going to be present. Zana told him that, a few days before, the Governor had instructed Abdullah to go to Hockail and collect her jewellery. Abdullah had not done so. He had been arrested and imprisoned, in a jail five hours' drive from Taiz. Zana was exultant. She had heard her husband had cried solidly since he had been flung in a cell. "Let him rot," she said.

Ahmed had also been flung into prison for three days, but, according to Miriam, when the Governor heard that Jim was coming, he had been released. His crime, apparently, had been that he was supposed to be plotting to get a British passport, which he was entitled to do. The husbands had reported him as a troublemaker and, on their word, he had been jailed.

The meeting with the Governor lasted three hours. Often he put his head in his hands and groaned. Nadia's husband said that he was keen to go to Britain still, for the sake of his children and also because he liked his wife, in spite of everything. In the lengthy discussion, it appeared that it was just possible that Mohammed was entitled to a British passport. His father, Gohad, was a British citizen, and so, if Mohammed had been born after he naturalised, he could be a British subject by descent.

Zana's husband, weeping in his cell, might just be persuaded to sign release papers so that she could apply for an exit visa. As she was the wronged person in his crime of failing to bring her jewellery, she could forgive him and have him released — if he would sign on the dotted line.

The thing that came over most during the meeting was the utter desperation of the Governor to get the Muhsens out of his country. Jim told the family afterwards: "You are home and dry. They want you to go as much as you want to leave."

That night, the Home Office contacted Gohad in Birmingham, to ask him for details about both his naturalisation and the true birth date of his son. Gohad stalled and would tell them nothing. It was yet another last-ditch attempt to ensure that his son and troublesome daughter-in-law never landed back on his doorstep. But unfortunately for him, the Embassy already had the details it needed. Gohad had recently sent in an application to the Embassy for another son he had in Yemen to join him in Britain. Sitting in the Consular department in Sana'a was the photocopy of Gohad's passport.

The Consul despatched another telegram, asking for a few more details relating to the boy. If the passport was granted, Mohammed could travel to Britain as a genuine passport holder. It would mean that Nadia could leave with her children.

When I told Zana this, she was despondent. "What about me?" she asked plaintively. "No matter what I say to Abdullah he will not sign the permission papers. Even if he is in prison, he will not disobey his father." All I could tell her was what Jim had told me; that certain highly placed officials in Sana'a were working behind the scenes. Perhaps her husband's permission was not going to be necessary.

I had another desperate phone call from Miriam. Mohammed had been instructed by Gohad that under no circumstances was he to leave Yemen. Even were his passport now to be granted, he would not use it. It seemed an impasse.

But in Sana'a, the Government decided that day that enough was enough. The Foreign Minister, Doctor Ala-Riyani, called in the British Ambassador. His country was fed-up to the back teeth of the situation, and he had been called upon to conclude matters as swiftly as possible. Zana's husband, languishing in jail, was to be released and brought to Sana'a. There he would be forced either to sign the permission slip allowing his wife to go home, or divorce her. There would be no question of a court case; he would simply have to say in front of witnesses: "I divorce thee, I divorce thee, I divorce thee." That took care of Zana.

If Nadia's husband was eligible for a passport, the Government was going to make sure he used it — even if it meant he only landed in Britain, then came home. If he was not entitled to the passport, he too would be forced to divorce Nadia.

The high-level Government intervention, which Jim admitted was "way out of proportion for the case" meant, he thought, that release was literally days away for the girls. Miriam would have to leave the country by Wednesday, 2 March, for her visa had expired and would not again be renewed. But, said Dr Ala-Riyana, that tied in well — it had always been intended that the mother would leave in advance of her daughters. They would follow shortly after.

Everyone's spirits soared at the news, although the girls, after so many weeks of false hopes, still feared they would never leave Yemen. I talked to Jim and to Miriam, and we decided Paris would be a good place to wait until she could be reunited with her daughters again. Miriam was desperate, she said, not to go home, for she knew she would be besieged by the media, and did not feel she could cope with it. She had also been told by Jim that she could wreck her daughters' chances of release, even at this late hour, by talking about her version of events in Taiz. She could not guarantee that she would not let something which would be viewed as detrimental to Yemen slip out, even to a friend, who then might be interviewed by reporters. Miriam was told not to breathe a word to anyone about Paris, and she promised faithfully to keep silent.

On Wednesday, 24 February, Jim was told that an elderly British man in Sana'a would have to be repatriated immediately due to ill-health and that he would need to be accompanied on the flight. Jim leapt at the chance. In London he would be able to lobby the Home Office to issue Mohammed's passport and, once he had that in his hands, Nadia's predicament would be over. He arrived in London, after a delayed flight of 36 hours' duration on Friday, 26 February, and went immediately to the Home Office. There was still no answer, he was told. The Foreign Office

Consular department, however, promised to do its own investigation and to have the answer ready for Jim's return to Yemen early the following week.

I met up with Jim on the Saturday morning. He said he was very optimistic of a speedy conclusion to the whole affair. "If it goes on much longer I don't know who will have the nervous breakdown first, Miriam or me," he said.

He had been researching a lot into the whole subject of brides in Yemen. He said that if, as had been repeatedly alleged, Zana and Nadia were married off for £1,300 apiece, the boys' fathers had got the "bargain of the week". Normally in Yemen the price was several thousands more.

He told me about "family law" in Yemen, which allows children once they achieve "majority" to be married. Age is calculated differently in Yemen family law. It is by "hagria", a shorter length of time than a year. It appeared, under this law, that Nadia's marriage at the age of 14 was illegal, she was only 15 hagria years old, and a girl has to be 16 hagrias old; the boy 15 hagrias. Both boys were under age when married. "But in the tribal villages of Mokbana, no law touches the families," said Jim. "They do just what they please and nobody is any the wiser."

He was currently working on another two lost British children cases, both girls from Birmingham: 11-year-old Nicola Razzack and a 12-year-old-girl who cannot be named because she is a ward of court. When Nicola was five years old she went with her mother, Maria, baby sister and Yemeni father on holiday to his country. Once there, Mr Mohammed Razzak, according to his now estranged wife, tried to force them to stay. In 1982, he finally allowed his wife to go home with their baby, but insisted that Nicola remain to be cared for by his parents in the village of Mayga. Her mother succeeded in getting Nicola made a ward of court, but the British ruling held no sway in Yemen. Again, as with the Muhsen girls, the Embassy had been given no information as to where the village was, and it is not shown on any maps. "Her mother is worried that when she reaches 12 or 13, she will be married. We would like to help, but first we have to find the child."

He had managed to locate the 12-year-old, who also had a mother in Birmingham desperate to have her daughter home.

This girl was living in Al-Rokab, in Mokbana — Jim said we must have passed the village on our way to Ashube. After many days of telephone calls, he had talked to the girl on the phone. "She told me she was happy living with her grandmother," said Jim. "She did not want to go home because she said her mother and stepfather used to beat her. She said that she was betrothed to a 16-year-old boy, and wanted to marry him. I mentioned that she would be breaking family law, but it did not seem to mean much to her." It had also been discovered that the 12-year-old's father had been granted custody of his daughter in Birmingham before taking the child to his home country.

Jim said that he had now learned much about the role of a wife in Yemen society. Little girls of ten and 11 were often to be seen in Yemen, dressed completely in black, he said, the sign that they were betrothed. When they reached puberty they were married to their bridegrooms. A little extra snippet was that it is risky in Sana'a, if a woman wears blue shoes — it is the sign of a prostitute. The wife's role is subservient: for example, she is expected to provide sex for her husband, any time, day or night. Jim also told me that stoning to death for adultery was extremely popular in the country, particularly in Taiz and Mokbana.

We had a long chat about Paris, even planning an out-of-the-way hotel for Miriam to avoid detection by journalists. Ben and I would arrive before her, and wait with her. When I went home, I had a call from Muriel. Miriam's son, Mohammed, had just told her that Anne Sufi knew about Paris. Mrs Sufi, we knew, was in close contact with several journalists and might pass on the information. So again our plans had to change. The situation was rapidly assuming the proportions of a nightmare, or more realistically, a farce.

Chapter Nineteen

The deadline for Miriam's return from Yemen, 2 March, was three days away when I heard from Jim's deputy, Bob Jackson. He had received a curious message from the Ministry of Foreign Affairs that "Miriam plus one daughter are to be given permission
to travel".

Jim was still en route back to Sana'a, and Bob had been unable to get the Ministry to explain its announcement more fully. He thought it might simply mean that one girl would be allowed to accompany her mother to the airport in Taiz, or to travel with her to Sana'a. Of course it could mean that either Zana or Nadia was free.

On Monday, 1 March, after consulting with Robin Lustig, *The Observer*'s news editor, I booked tickets for Miriam and one Miss Muhsen under assumed names. This was necessary to prevent any other journalist from discovering through checking in-flight lists, that the women were on their way home. We had decided on Rome as a destination; Ben and I would travel early on Tuesday to meet them.

Later that day, our plans changed again. Jim called to say that only Miriam was coming out, the message given to Bob had been wrong. He said that he hoped, although he could not guarantee, that the girls would still be following their mother within two weeks. It was even possible that the girls might follow within a couple of days, he said, but he expected a fortnight was more likely. I wondered what it would be like with a desperate Miriam living in a small hotel in Rome, and after further discussion with Robin Lustig we finally thought London would be a better place for Miriam to endure a more lengthy wait. At least she would be easily able to telephone her daughters.

Tickets were cancelled and changed; Miriam, as "Mrs Mary Bond" would be travelling Lufthansa to Paris, then transferring to arrive in Heathrow, where I would meet her. The travel agents, who were fully aware of Mrs Bond's true identity, and had been following the story closely, thought her alias was hilarious. They referred to her as "007". As it turned out, however, our precautions were wholly necessary. As soon as Miriam left Taiz on Sunday 28 February, the commander, Abdul Walli, informed all journalists who called — the girls remember there were at least eight — that she was about to fly out of Yemen.

Jim was inundated with telephone calls, demanding to know Miriam's whereabouts. He was able to read from a letter written by Miriam the previous month that she did not wish any details of either her own or her daughters' travel arrangements to be made known.

Miriam's flight from Paris was delayed. I waited for her at Heathrow's Terminal Four, wondering whether she had decided to hop on a plane direct to Birmingham from Charles de Gaulle airport. She was the last one off the flight; her luggage had been mislaid. It was two hours more before it was found, but Miriam was in good spirits, if worried about how her daughters would fare in the clutches of the commander, Abdul Walli. "He wants Zana as his wife," she said. "He was good to me and to the girls at first, but then he wrecked it all. He gave me a gold watch and asked if he could marry her. I have told the girls to keep away from him, but I don't know if they will now that I am not there."

The attraction of the commander's house was a telephone. Very few people in Taiz were willing to let the girls into their homes, even though they were sympathetic to their plight. The fear of coming to the notice of National Security was too great. However, a dentist and his wife had shown the sisters kindness, and had promised they could use their phone to receive incoming calls. A woman who ran a wives' refuge in the town had also offered the girls help.

I suggested to Miriam that she stay in a hotel in London. She was horrified; she dreaded hotels, she said. "It will be too

posh. I don't like strangers," she said. I said that I would book
in with her, but she shook her head. "Can't I come home with
you?" she begged. "It's all right at your home, and I feel safe
there." I had expected this; I knew I had really made a mistake
at Christmas in having her at home. But Paul and I had talked
about it and decided that it was probably better Miriam being
at home for a short while — we hoped no more than a few days
— than me having to live in a hotel with her.

When her luggage was finally retrieved, we joined the rush
hour traffic back to London. On the journey, I emphasised to
Miriam how important it was that she did not speak to anyone
who might pass on information to other journalists. "I know. I
won't say anything. I don't want to say anything until the girls
are back. Jim has told me if I start talking about the Yemenis,
and what I think of them, it will mean they won't come home,"
she said. I told her that I thought it would be very unwise for
her even to talk to her close friend, Mrs Sufi. "Oh, I've got to
tell her I am home, she is my friend," she cried. I explained
that Mrs Sufi was too closely in contact with other newspapers,
but Miriam only shrugged. I had to make the point clear; I said
that the paper had instructed me that if any news "leaked out"
via Miriam, then we would no longer foot her daughters' living
expenses. Miriam would have to find another newspaper to help
her.

That made her sit up and listen. She promised to keep quiet
until her daughters were home. To put her mind at rest about
Mrs Sufi being worried about her, I stopped the car at a phone
box and contacted the office. Robin Lustig agreed that the best
idea would be for himself to telephone Mrs Sufi with a message
from Miriam that she was safe, out of Yemen, and staying with
me. He would also emphasise to Mrs Sufi that on the Consul's
instructions, Miriam would be saying nothing publicly until she
was reunited with her daughters. He added that Mr Quirke had
called him to enquire of Miriam's whereabouts. Robin had told
him, fairly truthfully, that he did not know.

I called Paul. His afternoon sleep — although the company
lawyer at TV-AM, he was acting as a cameraman during the
strike — had been wrecked by a string of telephone calls. Mrs
Sufi, told by Mr Quirke that Miriam had left Yemen, had called,

demanding to speak to her friend. Mr Quirke had also called. He wanted to know if Miriam was at home, or in Larnaca. Journalists we had never heard of had phoned with offers of money. A German magazine was willing to pay £50,000 for Miriam. BBC and ITN wanted to interview her. Jim had also phoned saying that he had been flooded by calls. It looked like the circus was in full swing again. Paul's temper was not improved when I told him that Miriam was insisting that she come home. He had known that in all likelihood we would have our house-guest again, but his reaction was not one of overweening joy.

Back in the car, I told Miriam about the various offers and pleas for interviews. "I don't want no interviews," she said. "I just want my kids."

When we arrived home in the early evening, there had been yet more calls. Paul had switched on our answer-phone, and we decided it was best to leave it on so that all calls could be monitored. Everyone knew Miriam had left the Yemen, but no one knew where she was, and that was the way that we wanted it to stay.

Paul and I had been meant to be going on a ski-ing holiday on 5 March. I had not yet cancelled my place, hoping that it was just conceivable that the girls would come out on Thursday or Friday. On Friday, 4 March, however, Jim called to say it would be at least another week. He had heard that Mohammed would not be granted a passport; the Home Office had decreed that he was not eligible for one. Now both girls would have to get divorced. He had been told that this would be happening on Monday, 7 March. The Ministry of Foreign Affairs had promised that it would not be a "normal divorce" — that is one taking several years.

Miriam was impatient and extremely demanding. She scarcely uttered a word to Paul, and treated me rather as her slave — expecting meals to be cooked, her cigarettes bought, and a constant stream of videos fetched. She was content to sit in front of the television, watching films and drinking beer. I longed to tell her to get her own cup of tea, or suggest to her that a "thank-you" would not go amiss when presented with a meal. I could not afford to offend her though, and she knew it.

On 5 March, I drove Paul to the airport. Miriam had insisted on coming along; she said she was bored. On the way back, I wondered how much longer I could put up with her — I thought I might start sleepwalking and inadvertently murder her. Her other children and grandchild were arriving the next day to visit their mother. I considered just packing a suitcase and leaving them the house.

It was not a happy evening. Miriam had been unable to speak to the girls when she telephoned the Taiz dentist's home. The girls, he told her, had not arrived that day. Miriam rapidly became distraught. She felt she had to contact her daughters with the news that they were to go for their divorces on Monday. At her insistence, the good dentist went to the flat where the girls were staying to find them. Miriam phoned him back an hour later only to hear he had been unsuccessful. The girls were nowhere to be found. She was now verging on hysterics, and I did my best to calm her. It seemed to me that if the Ministry of Foreign Affairs had decided the divorces would take place on Monday, then the girls would be found. After several hours, she began to calm down, and I crept upstairs to our phone in the bedroom to speak to Muriel Wellington, who was still looking after Miriam's son. Mohammed, the 15-year-old boy, had spoken to his mother the previous day and said that he wanted to stay in London with her. Miriam had said: "That's OK, son." Once I had got over reeling from the woman's cheek, I thought that perhaps the presence of Mohammed on the spare couch might make his mother more reasonable.

The children descended *en masse* the next day. The grandchild, a three-year-old girl called Lena, ran wild for seven hours, breaking things and screaming blue murder if she was not allowed her own way. Aisha, her mother, on several occasions attempted to reprimand her, but was shouted down by Miriam. In desperation I phoned Ben, who lived just a mile away and said I was about to commit a massacre. I had cooked a meal which I served to them, and then fled to a curry house where I met up with Ben. Very reluctantly he agreed to come back and talk to the family — by that stage I doubted whether I could look at them in a civil fashion.

Surprisingly, the house was not only still standing, but looked neat. I thanked Aisha for clearing up, but Miriam interrupted: "I did it."

"Good God," I said, and that seemed to be the turning-point. Miriam suddenly became reasonable for the majority of the time. There was further good news— Mohammed had decided not to stay. He had thought his sisters were coming out very quickly, and that they naturally would be living in our home with his mother. When Miriam had told him that the girls were being met by us somewhere in Europe, he had opted to return to Birmingham. They left at midnight for home. Mohammed was now staying with Aisha. He felt he had intruded upon Mrs Wellington's hospitality too long.

The following day, Miriam tried continually to get through to the girls, without success. Again I tried to calm her, reasoning that if this was indeed the day when the divorces were happening the girls would be busy, probably at the office of the Governor of Taiz. Finally, in the evening, she reached them. There had been no summons to the Governor's office; no Government intervention.

But the girls' absence of the previous two days was explained. Zana told her mother that their uncle, Muthana Muhsen's brother, whom Miriam had met, had decided to help them. On Saturday he had taken his nieces out of Taiz for a day by the seaside. There he convinced them that he was their knight in shining armour, and he had arranged for them to see a judge in Taiz the following day.

Both girls went to the judge's home, and Zana was again asked if she was truly willing to leave her son behind. "Of course I said 'yes'," declared Zana. "Then he said to me that my divorce was no problem, I could have it that week, then go home. But he told me that Jim could not be present; they did not want the British Consul interfering.

"Nadia said she still wanted her children, and he said he would personally make sure she got them, if she went for divorce. He said that Nadia's husband could be convinced that it was in everyone's best interests that he divorce her. He said it may take a few more weeks, but it is was what we both wanted."

Miriam beseeched Nadia to abandon her children, saying it was the only way she would be allowed to leave. She felt, as I did, that the judge's promise was possibly simply a delaying tactic. But the girls were adamant. They added that they were now back on speaking terms with the commander, who once more was being very helpful to them. But he had asked them not to call the British Consul. "We do this the Yemeni way," he had told the girls. "You are Yemeni women, not British. It does not concern the British Consul."

I contacted Jim with the latest news. He felt that the girls were probably being led up the garden path, and asked that they contact him. His message was relayed by Miriam, but the girls did not respond.

On 12 March, the day that Paul returned from ski-ing, we heard that Nadia's husband had refused to divorce her, in spite of various figures in authority applying pressure. But Jim by then had received further communication from the Ministry of Foreign Affairs. Zana's husband was to be released from jail. He had agreed to divorce her. Nadia was to be given a lawyer, appointed on behalf of the Ministry, for her divorce hearing. The girls were to be given the name of the lawyer, who lived in Taiz, and told to go and see him immediately.

Miriam could hardly wait to tell the girls the news. But they sounded more frightened than pleased. Zana told me why. "We are not used to talking to important people. We don't know what we would say to a lawyer," she said. Then Nadia said the commander had told them if they got a Government lawyer, her husband would get an even more important lawyer to represent him. When I told Jim this piece of information, he pointed out: "Nadia's husband is not capable of buying a paper bag, let alone getting a decent lawyer. He has no money."

It took two days of telephone calls to convince the girls to attempt to see the Taiz lawyer. Luck was not on their side when they did try — he was in Saudi Arabia, said his family. They did not know when he would be back.

On Friday, 18 March, Zana told us that the commander had promised her a divorce on Monday. He had visited her father-in-law, who had returned from Saudi Arabia, and repaid her bride-money. On Monday she would be free, but would have to give up her son. Zana said she did not care. "Look, I've got to get out of here," she told me. "He (her son) will be OK. His grandparents will look after him. He will forget me." There was silence for a few moments, then she gave a deep sigh, and was crying. "Maybe one day he will come to England. He will forgive me."

Jim had told us that he had discovered the lawyer was back in Taiz. At his request I urged Nadia to go with her sister as soon as possible to see the man. She told me: "I know if I go to the lawyer and do it the Government way I will lose my children. I don't want to do that."

Miriam grabbed the phone and bellowed at her daughter that she would lose them anyway, in all likelihood. "Jim says go to the lawyer, and the Government have promised you will be home very quick. Do it."

Nadia finally gave in to pressure, and promised her mother she would. She told her that the reason her husband was refusing to co-operate was that his father, Gohad, in Birmingham, was in almost daily contact with him by telephone, instructing his son not to grant Nadia the divorce. Jim, when this was relayed, promised to pass it on to the Ministry of Foreign Affairs. Miriam wanted to pay Gohad a visit and persuade him to change his mind.

On Sunday, 20 March, Zana had more news. "The commander has waved this bit of paper at me. I think it is my divorce paper, but he will not tell me," she said. "He says I will know tomorrow. But he wants me to wait until May when he is coming to England, so I can come out with him."

After much shouting, Miriam felt she had managed to persuade Zana not to listen to the commander. She wished her daughter well the next day. "Just get the divorce, wait for Nadia, and come home," she begged.

Assuming all was going well in Taiz on Monday I drove Miriam up to Birmingham. We had arranged to see Gohad at his place of work, a components factory in Tyseley, Birmingham. His boss, Mr Don Hammond, had agreed to see Miriam and me and to try to help bring the situation to an end.

Miriam explained that she had talked to a lawyer, which was true, and that Gohad could be answerable to several criminal charges under the Sexual Offences Act, namely abduction of an under-age girl, and conspiring to detain an under-age girl against the will of her guardian — Miriam. She said that she would be prepared not to press the charges if only Gohad would co-operate and tell his son to let her daughter go. Acting on Jim's advice, she said that if his son really did not want to divorce Nadia, then why would he not allow her to travel to England, keeping their children as surety?

Mr Hammond, the managing director of the company, Thomas Eaves Ltd, turned out to be a special police constable. He listened attentively to what Miriam had to say, and then said he would try to get Gohad into his office to talk things through. He insisted that Miriam would have to restrain herself. She had told him she wanted to kill his employee.

Mr Hammond returned a few minutes later — alone. Gohad had, for the first time in his working life, gone home without telling his foreman about ten minutes before we arrived. Someone had obviously tipped him off. Mr Hammond said that if we were prepared to wait another day, he would tackle Gohad in the morning.

Miriam went to stay with Muriel Wellington, and I booked into a hotel. The next morning, Mr Hammond called. Gohad had agreed to see me — not Miriam — that night at his home. I was not too keen on this. I thought it highly unlikely that Gohad would actually see me at his home. I would probably be left standing on the doorstep shouting through the letter-box. Also, I was well aware that I was hardly his favourite journalist, and it was just possible he could turn nasty. I told Mr Hammond all this, adding that I thought Gohad would be far more reasonable if speaking to me in front of his boss. Mr Hammond promised to see what he could do, and rang off.

At 5 p.m. he called again. He had apparently told Gohad that just to make sure he talked to me, he would accompany me to the evening meeting. Gohad had blanched, then cancelled the appointment. Mr Hammond had pressed him until the man had agreed to see me at his office, with his boss, the next day. I groaned — not another night kicking my heels in Birmingham. Mr Hammond suggested I could always just drop in, that evening, before Gohad went home at 5.30 p.m. It was worth a try.

I arrived within 20 minutes. Mr Hammond fetched Gohad, and his employee came into the office, his face wreathed in smiles, and desperately anxious to help Nadia. "My daughter," he cried. "Nobody loves her more."

He listened carefully to what I had to say. When I mentioned that I knew he had been phoning his son with instructions every day, his smile slipped momentarily. He really started to take interest when I mentioned the name of the commander, Abdul Walli, and that the Government were now prepared to back Nadia in a divorce hearing. "Think of the shame on your family that the Government should appoint a lawyer against your son," I said.

Gohad thought. "I will send Nadia the money to buy her air ticket," he said. "I will call my son and tell him to let Nadia go." Whether he would or not, I did not know, but his promise was more than I had hoped for.

I left for London, leaving Miriam for a few days, so that she could see her other children.

Gohad did call his son. He told him to go to the British Embassy to try to get a visitor's visa to travel with Nadia to England. But we were not to know he had done this for another week.

When I got home, I had a call from Miriam. Zana's divorce, she had been told, had not gone through. Apparently the commander had been told of a story which had appeared in *The Observer* the previous Sunday, that she was to be divorced. He had cancelled the proceedings in a fit of pique. He had also told the girls that he forbade them to speak to Jim ever again, and warned them that anything they said to their mother was being immediately broadcast. The girls believed every word he said. There had been an attempt the previous week to get the girls into a hotel, out of his clutches. We had arranged for money to be made available to them at the Banque d'Indo-Suez in Taiz. The girls had bragged that they would be moving into a hotel to the commander and he had immediately terrified them out of such an action by promising he would have them arrested if they did any such thing.

They were eating out of his hand. He told them that they had to do everything he said, and he would get them home. If they disobeyed in any way, he would see to it that they never left the Yemen. They had become as much prisoners in Taiz as they had been in the villages.

Ahmed and Miriam, February 1988.

Chapter Twenty

The only faint glimmer of hope was that the girls were still responding to their mother's pleas that they should contact the lawyer. Again, however, when they did call him, it was only to be told that he was away in Sana'a — his family did not know where he was, but promised they would pass on the message that the girls wanted to speak to him, should he contact his wife.

On Sunday, 27 March, Jim called to say that the girls' divorces were going ahead in the morning. The lawyer was in Taiz looking for the sisters. He was to take them to the Governor's office early on Monday and, if all went according to plan, the girls would be home in two days. I almost said "Ha, ha."

I contacted Miriam and told her the news, but did not mention the two days' hope. She had been promised her daughters were coming home too many times. I did tell her, however, that she had to get through to her daughters and tell them to call the lawyer immediately, that they could get their divorces. She was delighted. All that day she tried calling the girls at the commander's house, only to be told they were not there.

She tried on Monday, then phoned me. She was convinced her daughters were at the house, but would not talk to her. She asked that Ben and I travel to Birmingham the following day to try to reason with them by telephone. We thought it was worth a try.

At the appointed hour, 2 p.m. on 29 March, Miriam dialled the number from her temporary home. A man answered and said the girls were not there. Miriam screamed at him to get her daughters, but he laughed softly, and put the phone down.

I dialled the number again; Miriam was too distraught. I heard the sound of children's voices, and, I thought, Zana, in the background — but neither sister would come to the phone.

It sunk into Miriam that her daughters had been persuaded not to talk to her. She began to scream and lash out, then she completely broke down, sobbing: "What are they doing to me?"

The couple called a doctor, and Miriam was given tranquillizers. Ben and I tried to reassure her that the girls were probably not there. We urged her to try contacting the girls in the morning.

The couple told us before we left that they did not know how much longer they could tolerate Miriam. "Of course we are sorry for her, but she is so ungrateful, never lifting a finger and ordering our children around like her servants," they said. I knew just what they meant.

On the way back to London that night Ben and I both expressed the wish that we had never started the story. We felt everyone was going round in circles, and doubted whether the girls would ever leave. The Yemenis had everyone over a barrel: Miriam bound not to utter a word in case she jeopardised the girls' chances, the Embassy saying nothing for the same reason, and the fathers in Birmingham directing operations by telephone, aided most successfully by the commander who would probably end up marrying Zana.

The next morning, back at work, I called Jim with the latest news. He said that he would go to the girls in Taiz at the weekend unless he heard from them in the next few days. That afternoon, The couple phoned with the news that Miriam had finally managed to talk to the girls by telling the man who laughed at her that she was very ill. To make her point clearer, they had snatched the phone and screamed at the man that Miriam had to go into hospital. The man, who had denied that either girl was present, stopped laughing, and within a few seconds, Nadia came fearfully on to the telephone.

"Miriam really laid it on about how ill she was, and how she was going to have to go into hospital if the girls did not do as she said," they recalled. "I had a go at Nadia as well, and she started to cry. I told her they could have been home yesterday if they only had gone to the lawyer.

She promised that she would call Jim. I could tell she meant it."

The message had finally got home. Jim reported the next day that he had had a lengthy conversation with Zana. Gohad had telephoned the previous week, and Nadia's husband had agreed he would travel to Sana'a on Saturday, 2 April, so that he could be interviewed by Jim for a one-month visa. He had promised in front of the Governor of Taiz, and, apparently a judge, that if his visa was not granted, he would give Nadia permission to travel alone after Ramadan — May 17.

In this call she revealed that in fact she had been divorced on 6 March — the day when her uncle took her to the judge. "I could not say anything before in case Mum said anything to the newspapers," said Zana. She still had her son with her, but was expecting that he would be taken from her any day.

She told Jim: "I will be free to leave on June 6 — three months after my divorce. I have to wait three months to prove I am not pregnant — it is the Islamic way."

Jim said that Zana sounded positively chirpy and absolutely confident that if everyone did everything the commander's way, they would be home in the first half of June. Nadia, of course, might be able to travel before her. The message that both she and Nadia were desperate to be conveyed to their mother was that they were "OK". Miriam, they said, must not worry any longer.

Once again, I acted as go-between. Miriam was pleased with the news that the girls had obeyed her, but she had had too many false hopes to really believe her daughters were coming home on a given date.

It was just as well we had all learned to be sceptical of promised meetings. That weekend, no one materialised in Jim's office. The next week, with only days to go before the start of Ramadan, the girls vanished. By Wednesday, Miriam was again on the point of a breakdown. The laughing gentleman had told her that the girls were in Sana'a with the commander. He gave her a telephone number there, which she tried with no success. Then Jim had another call from Zana — they would see him in his office on 10 March, a Sunday.

Once more, the day came and went with no sign of either the girls or Nadia's husband. Two days later Jim had another call from Zana. She sounded penitent — Nadia would see him on Wednesday morning. They were all in Sana'a with the commander.

Her call had been in response to another talk with her mother. After days of trying the Sana'a telephone number, Miriam had finally got through to her daughters. "Do you bloody well want to come home?" she screamed at Zana. Her eldest daughter had calmly told her that the reason they had not been around was that the commander had been taking them out. Miriam hardly ever got angry with her two girls; Zana was shocked into silence.

"Yes, Mum, but we have got to do what he wants," she whispered. Only half-acting, Miriam went into a swoon. Muriel grabbed the phone and shouted to Zana: "Your mum has fainted, phone us back."

Zana was on the phone, in tears, within seconds. Jim would be contacted at once, she promised — and this time she obeyed.

The long-awaited interview in Jim's office was a disappointment. Nadia arrived with Mohammed, her husband, and her brother, Ahmed. Nadia insisted on taking Zana's British passport, and Ahmed took his own. Nadia would scarcely open her mouth, beyond saying that everything was "OK". Jim said: "She was there for about an hour and spoke six words. At one point I said, 'Look, Nadia, what the hell is going on?' She would not answer me. I filled up her husband's application form for a visitor's visa — but he had not got the relevant papers. I said they would have to get and get them — Nadia said they were in Taiz."

Nadia and the men left, promising to come back at the weekend. Jim left for home at screaming pitch. That afternoon he had another phone call from Zana. The girl sounded desperate, and did not speak for long. "Don't tell Mummy but I am coming home soon," she said. "I have got to come very soon because Mummy is so sick."

Jim said: "I asked her what about her exit visa — I knew that she must now have been given her passport by Nadia. Zana said: 'Don't worry about my exit visa — that's OK.' I said what about the Ministry of Foreign Affairs — did they know what was going on? She said that was OK too. All she would tell me was that I was not to worry, she would be home soon. She said that the previous day she had signed an official document saying that she agreed to leave behind her son. She could not tell me any more. She insisted that I say nothing to Miriam. She said: 'I will come home, then I will phone Eileen and tell her where I am.'"

From his brief chat to Zana, Jim surmised that she was going to get out of the country by a devious route. As it happened, on Thursday, 14 April, he had received a visa application from a Yemeni man who worked in the office of the Governor of Taiz to travel the following day. The man had not properly completed the form — it was still in Jim's tray on Friday. He thought it was possible that this man was Zana's exit visa. "I think when he travels, we may find Zana with him," he said..

Four days later, on 19 April, we had the news we had waited months for. Early in the morning, Jim had a call at the Embassy from a Mr Basha, an official in the Ministry of Foreign Affairs. "Zana Muhsen is free to travel," he told Jim. "We have her divorce papers in front of us, and the paper she has signed renouncing any claim to her son. She can leave when she wants."

Jim picked himself up off the floor and reached for a bottle of beer he had kept specially for this purpose. Mr Basha was asking for Zana's British passport so that it could be stamped with an exit visa. Jim had to explain, much to the man's displeasure, that the passport was now in Miss Muhsen's own possession in Taiz. He promised that he would contact Zana at the earliest opportunity.

"Do that," said Mr Basha. "If she comes up to Sana'a tomorrow, she should be able to leave by the end of this week." He added that the Ministry were now fully aware of the commander's involvement, and even knew that Zana had received 6,000 rials in her divorce settlement — roughly half her bride-price — from her ex-husband the previous week.

All that there now remained to do was to get a message through to Zana to come to Sana'a. But when Jim phoned the commander's house, the phone was put down on him. Miriam finally got through on Wednesday. Zana already knew about the homecoming. It was set for two days' time. "She sounded sad, though," said her mother. "I asked what was wrong, but she said she could not tell me."

On Thursday, Jim called telling me that Zana was now booked on Yemenia flight number IY748, leaving Sana'a at 9 a.m. on 22 April, arriving Gatwick Airport at 5.40 p.m. He had still not heard from the girl — all his information was coming from the Yemeni Ministry.

That Thursday night, the commander took Zana to Sana'a, but she was under instruction not to call Jim. The commander still wanted the British Consul to have no involvement. There remained a problem — it was now Ramadan and the slow bureaucracy of the Yemen was now proceeding at a snail's pace. Zana had still to get her exit visa. The commander's men scoured the city for the proper official, who was trying to eat and relax after a day's fasting. It was 2.30 a.m. on Friday before the man was found and the visa stamped in Zana's British passport.

She slept little. That afternoon she had left behind Marcus, her son. He was temporarily staying with Nadia, but his grandfather, Abdul Khada, would be fetching him. Zana said: "It was funny, he seemed to know. He was with me and the commander in the car, and I got out to leave him. Normally he would have screamed for me, but he just grabbed at the commander's sleeve, as if to say 'She's no use to me any more.' I have made myself hard, but I am like any other mother leaving her baby. Imagine how I felt."

At 4.30 a.m. on Friday, Nadia called to wish her good luck. Marcus was screaming in the background. Zana said: "I asked her why she had phoned — was it just to hear him cry? Then I put the phone down."

She was driven to the airport by the commander, who had dressed in his military-style uniform. He handed her a ticket, and her passport. She sat waiting for the flight, thinking of her mother and Nadia.

One person saw her leave — Jim. He had to be at the airport to see a friend off. He scoured the terminal building, then saw the commander standing over the girl. Worried that his presence might cause trouble, he left.

At 7.40 a.m. British time, he phoned me. "Zana is on the plane. She is dressed in white from head to toe," he told me. I called Miriam, who had been crying all night, praying that her daughter would get on the plane. We arranged that she should come to the newspaper office by 1 p.m.

At work, there was much to be planned. There was the strong possibility that the news of Zana's arrival would leak to the rest of the Press. Not only were we anxious to have an exclusive, but we knew that neither Zana nor Miriam could cope with a battery of cameras and reporters when she walked through into Gatwick's Arrivals Hall. I called Gatwick's public relations office to ask if they could either allow Ben and me, or Miriam, on to the airport tarmac, so that Zana could be met. All they could offer was that Zana would be met by an airport official, escorted through customs and immigration, then onto the public concourse. She would be mobbed, we thought. The public relations office then said they would tip off the airport's police, so that she would be given a protected passage through any media throng.

When Miriam arrived, we discussed the plan. Zana had specifically asked her mother that there should be "no Press" on her arrival. Her mother thought she would be terrified — even with her police escort.

I tried the Foreign Office, asking if a representative could meet the girl at the aircraft. The cold answer came back: "I am afraid she is a dual national, a point we have made all along in this case. We cannot risk setting a precedent by meeting someone of dual nationality."

Shortly before 2 p.m., we heard that the news was out. Mr Tom Quirke had had a "hot tip", had picked up Anne Sufi and was speeding down the motorway. As he was being driven, he was apparently using a car phone to tip off other newspapers.

It was getting very late. We had to leave soon. We felt we had to risk relying on the police; there seemed nothing else to do.

Then Ben had a brainwave. We had talked earlier in the day about using a helicopter to take her off, but we did not know if Zana would have to go through the airport terminal first, or if she could just step into the helicopter from the plane. I called the public relations office back. They said they were sorry, but the helicopter pad was at a different terminal, and Zana would have to go through the main building. Ben rang the Linton helicopter company anyway. They gave us entirely different information. Zana could be met at the aircraft, escorted quickly through immigration and customs, without going through the terminal, then brought to the helicopter at the General Aviation Terminal, a short distance from where her plane would land. Miriam, Ben and I could be waiting for her in the helicopter.

We had no time to confirm anything. We literally leapt into the car with a portable telephone. On the way, as we were pushing and swerving through traffic, Robin Lustig telephoned. Everything was confirmed. We were to go straight to the General Aviation Terminal, where a representative from British Airways handling would meet us. The helicopter would land in a field some ten minutes from Brighton and a car would speed us to the town where we were booked into a hotel under false names.

We arrived at 5 p.m., only to hear that the aircraft was delayed until 7 p.m. The General Aviation Terminal was a wooden hut, with the "international departure lounge" squeezed along one side. It was like a scene from *Casablanca*. The small, rectangular windows looked onto the runways, old fan heaters keeping the room at sweltering point.

Jenny Hibbard, who was to meet Zana, made us tea and coffee. Miriam gave her a photo of Zana, a note explaining why Jenny was there, and Zana's birth certificate. At 6.40 p.m. Jenny came in and told us the plane was on its final approach — she left. We knelt on the sofas by the windows, with our noses pressed to the panes. Jenny had said it was a white and blue aircraft, and it would be flying in from the left. We stared at the blue skies until our eyes hurt.

Ten minutes later, our helicopter landed about 50 feet from us. We were escorted out to it and piled in our baggage. Ben wanted to get some pictures of the moment of reunion — he stayed outside, shaking with cold. The minutes ticked by. We wondered whether, in fact, at the last moment, she had not got on the flight.

Then we saw the white van, and inside, a girl in white Arab clothes, including a veil. Two police cars with flashing lights appeared. Miriam, sitting in the helicopter, began to cry. I helped her out; she was shaking so much I thought she would fall. From the other side of the van, to where we stood, Zana emerged. She and her mother ran into each other's arms, weeping, clutching each other as if they would never part. Ben and I greeted her too — she seemed in a state of shock — extremely withdrawn. She had only two pieces of hand-luggage. They were stowed into the rear of the helicopter and we all clambered in, with Ben in the front seat.

Zana stared at her mother. "I told you no Press," she hissed in a fury. "They are all right; you know them," said Miriam. Zana scowled and hissed again. I asked her if she felt all right. "Uh," she said. She took no interest in the scene from the air as we lifted off and circled the airport before moving out over the Sussex countryside.

She was like a mute. I asked if her flight had been all right. "Uh," again. Getting an interview out of this girl was going to be tricky. Ben, too, was having a hard time. Every time he pointed his camera at her she turned her head, whispering to her mother.

We landed in the field in the middle of nowhere. At the edge of it stood an ancient brick cottage, and there were children from the house waving at us. Zana ignored them. Without a word, she got out of the helicopter and began striding off. Her mother ran after her. A mini-cab driver met us at the gate. "This way," he said, and showed us to the car.

On the journey to Brighton we had expected Zana to be exclaiming over the country she had not seen for eight years. She did not utter a sound. Instead, Ben, Miriam and I were the ones making such comments as, "Look, a real gypsy caravan," and "What a big cow," receiving the response of "Uh."

She thought she was in London. She displayed some interest over the trees still lying broken after the hurricane of the winter of 1987. But when she began to talk it was only to ask when she was seeing her sisters and brother. We explained that we had to stay in a hotel until Sunday to avoid any other Press. She seemed unimpressed. "It is a posh one," Miriam pleaded. Zana was still unimpressed.

We booked into the Grand Hotel on the sea-front. Zana went straight to the room she was sharing with her mother, and tele-phoned Taiz. She said she was speaking to her sister, but as she was speaking in Arabic we did not know whether to believe her.

The meeting, April 1987.

Ben and I left them alone for an hour, then took them downstairs to dinner. Something was very wrong with Zana, and over the meal she began to thaw a little. She announced that was was going back to Taiz, soon.

Her mother wept. "Why? why?" she cried. "You hate it." "For Nadia," she said. "I have to go back, and then Nadia can come. I can't tell you any more — you would tell it to the press, then you would ruin everything."

She turned to Ben and I. "Everything I told you when we were in the villages was true. But in Taiz, it is a good life. I could have stayed, and I wanted to. It was only because I was worried about my mother that I have come to see her and my family.

Miriam and Zana, April 1988.

"I want to go back to Taiz and get a job. I will visit England when I want to. I am not sure I want to be a British woman anyway. I don't like the short skirts; it's disgusting."

She said that she was only eating that night, because she had a period. It was Ramadan, and menstruating women are permitted to eat. "I am unclean at the moment," she said. "I am a good Muslim now. I could recite you the Koran."

We could not understand the change in her. Even a few weeks ago she had been speaking of longing to be home, of rain, of going to discos. Now this sombre, bottled-up girl.

She glared at Miriam. "I am going to see my father. I want to see if he can look at me. I want you and my father to get back together again." This was more than Miriam could stand. "After what he did to you! After all the things you have said about him? Are you mad?"

"No," said Zana, coldly. "People change. Now I do not want revenge." Then she picked up her knife and fork. "How do I use these?" she asked, holding them awkwardly and in the wrong hands. "Can't I eat with my fingers?"

She was half-serious, half-joking. She asked if she could sit cross-legged on the carpet to have her food. She spurned any alcohol. "OI have never drunk," she said. Miriam said that in the morning they could go shopping for some warmer clothes. "I will not wear your clothes," Zana flashed back, angrily.

Over the course of dinner, her mood swung from cheeky to good humour to black depression. "My mind and my heart is

Miriam and Zana, April 1988.

in Taiz," she said. "Nadia could have come with me, but she is soft, she wouldn't leave her children. I am hard, my mother is soft. I have come to strengthen her."

Her ex-husband she dismissed as "skinny and with the mind of a child". "Nadia's husband is all right, though, but I am scared that unless I go back and push him he will not go to see Jim and get his visitor's visas. I am the only one who can save Nadia."

Her behaviour was breaking Miriam's heart. Late that night I heard them rowing, screaming at each other. As I worked through the night, I wondered what on earth was going on. Zana had said at dinner that she would have no problem in getting back to the Yemen. I wondered whether she had a return air ticket.

I finished at 4.30 a.m., had a bath, and waited until 7 a.m. to phone Jim. I told him of Zana's dramatic and bewildering talk and actions. I thought that she was probably in love with the commander, and going back to marry him. Jim agreed. "I think she may have a return ticket. The document case she was holding was the same one I have for a return ticket.

"Doesn't she realise that if she comes back and marries the man, that he will ship her back up to the village to have his babies? In a couple of years we will probably have a cry of despair from Zana of Mokbana."

Two hours later we knocked on the door. Zana was raring to go for a walk. Ben and I had just walked past the reception desk, when he was called back — there had been a phone call from a Commander Abdul Walli for Zana. She must have given her sister the phone number of the hotel. It would mean we would have to move. We could not risk the man tipping off any other journalists.

We did not tell Zana. I went back to the room to warn the office of our move, while Ben tried to photograph her and her mother on the beach. When she returned there was another call from the man. Miriam and I sat listening to a stream of Arabic. She finally flung down the phone. "Fuck, fuck, you cow," she screamed at Miriam, trying to kick her. "They know about the helicopter and the reporters. They know I was photographed. It has been on television." One of Ben's pictures from the previous night had been given to ITN and BBC. A Yemeni man in Birmingham had phoned to report her, and she was in trouble. "Don't you want Nadia back, you cow?"

I had to go back to work to write the front page story. Ben came in and confirmed that Zana had a return ticket — he had seen it while she was talking on the phone. Carmel Fitzsimmons, another *Observer* journalist, had arrived to "mind" Zana and Miriam while I worked. We delayed the move to another hotel, and warned the hotel security that reporters might come calling. They were very excited. They seemed keen to smuggle us out in the back of a lorry, but we hoped that such drama would not be necessary.

Carmel took mother and daughter shopping. Zana was interested in nothing for herself, but bought a little suit for her niece, Lena. She returned in a more cheerful state of mind, but desperate to go to Birmingham.

We hired a car and started the drive. But by the time we reached London Ben was nearly dead with exhaustion. We had only managed to sleep for an hour the previous night. I felt I was operating like a zombie. We could not travel any further. To Zana's fury, we decided to stay overnight at a London hotel and travel up the next day.

We did not know how she was going to react to *The Observer* article the next day. If she hated it, Ben and I were going to be very unpopular. We would have to leave. Carmel could take over, and a journalist from *The Observer*'s *M* magazine would arrive. The magazine had decided to run extracts from this book the following week.

We sat down to dinner. Zana was back in a good mood, giggling like a schoolgirl over the hotel's pianist and demanding a steak and kidney pie, "with lots of chips".

I had heard from a contact in Birmingham that her father had appeared on local television, saying that she was only staying for two weeks. She was on a mission to reconcile himself and Miriam, then she would return. He had had a call from Yemen, he said.

I challenged Zana, and she nodded. She was due back in the Yemen in a fortnight. Her only fear was that she would not get a visa. I had no doubts. What better public relations exercise for the Yemenis than the poor child bride loving her country so much she wanted to return?

She tried to convert us to Islam that night. With a mad gleam in her eye, born of missionary fervour, she told us what awaited us. "You will burn in the flames of hell," she said, spiking a chip with her fork. "Your agony will never end because when your skin has burned off, God will give you new skin. It will go on and on."

Brighton beach, April 1988.

Miriam asked about her father, after how he had made her and Nadia suffer. What would be his fate?

"He is a Muslim; he is saved. He will burn for a little bit, but Mohammed will intercede for him, and God will take him from the fire. But you bloody Christians, you have no hope."

It seemed to me that she had become some sort of fundamentalist. Then I remembered that the commander was a fundamentalist Muslim, one of the Muslim Brothers. It all fitted in.

After Miriam and Zana had gone to bed, Ben, Carmel and I sat talking about what her reaction was likely to be to the article. She had said at dinner that if there was anything about her in the Press she would "run back to Yemen to hide". She could do nothing on Sunday, for the Yemeni Embassy was shut —besides, she wanted to see her family in Birmingham the next day, and her reconciliation mission was not begun.

We need not have worried. She saw *The Observer* the next morning, read every word, very slowly, then announced: "It's very good. It says nothing bad about the Yemen."

Ben and I nearly collapsed with relief. We telephoned Sue Ryan, the magazine journalist, and told her we would meet her in Birmingham, then, leaving Carmel behind, we drove to the city Zana had dreamed of for eight years.

Miriam and Zana, April 1988.

Miriam waiting at Gatwick, April 1988.

Epilogue

She remembered Sparkbrook, pointing out her old haunts, even directing Ben through back roads. Miriam's other children tumbled out the door, and there were hugs and tears.

Her closest friend, Lynette Wellington, came into the room and Zana broke, sobbing and laughing. The two were like schoolgirls, giggling through the day at videos of Michael Jackson. "Ooh, isn't he lovely."

Ben and I left her alone, surrounded by her friends and family. Who knows what will happen now? Those who loved her were with her, and her hard self was distintegrating as her tears flowed.

Nadia

Zana

It seems that Nadia is a hostage, sitting in Taiz. Her return to Britain depends on Zana's future husband. She admitted to her friends that she has "fallen" for the commander. If she goes back, and if the commander has really got the power — apparently he was at school with the son of the President of the country — Nadia may return. They could be shuttling forever, one as a hostage, one as a wife. "Don't worry, Mum," said Zana in a softer moment. "I will be back in July for four whole months." It just so happens that that's when the commander is visiting his friend in Birmingham, Mr Adnan Saif.

Nadia has moved next door to the commander, so that she can receive bulletins from his sister by telephone. If her husband does not get his visa — and the Home Office have already refused him a settlement visa because the marriage was illegal — she may come to Britain, but would not be allowed to bring her children. It is doubtful that she would permanently leave them.

Zana may have a happily married life to the commander. She may be allowed to hop between the two countries. But the likelihood is she will end up back in Mokbana with the commander's other cast-off wives. She has lost her son; she is as lost in Britain as she was eight years ago when, at 15, she was dumped in a strange land.

Her mother has put her head in her hands and wept for her daughter. "I fear for her, I fear for her. She is blind to the dangers, and will not listen to me. I wonder if it was worth it all now."

Zana's father is rejoicing. The Yemeni community have taken him to their hearts. It is them against Britain. He always said he sold his daughters into marriage for their own good — to make them good Muslims rather than becoming prostitutes. He said just after Zana's return: "I will see my daughter. What happened was a long time ago. It is very cruel of her mother not to have allowed Zana to bring her baby to Britain. But then she was always like that. I have no regrets."